Praise for *Grandparenting Teens*

"I have known Mark for years, and I know that his heart and soul are all about helping families. *Grandparenting Teens* is a book full of life-changing stories that will inspire you to take an active approach in the lives of your grandchildren. Through these stories, Mark not only entertains readers but equips them with practical tips on how to be an involved grandparent."

—Paul Overstreet, country music Hall of Famer

"Mark does such an amazing job explaining and encouraging grandparents to take a more active role in the lives of our grandchildren. I truly believe that grandparents can make a profound difference in the lives of their grandchildren simply by being present and listening well."

—Amy Grant, winner of six Grammys and twenty-two Dove Awards

"I've known Mark for over forty-six years! He has always had an ability to communicate truth in a winsome and honest way. Here, Mark has struck a chord once again! Let this honest and biblical truth and instruction flow into your heart!"

—Steve Largent, NFL Hall of Famer and U.S. Congressman

"The best gift we can give our grandchildren is a meaningful relationship. *Grandparenting Teens* will make you laugh and encourage and equip you to love your grandchildren God's way, giving you the confidence you need to be present and active in their lives."

—Kirk Cameron, actor

"Mark has written many wonderful books through the years, but none is as timely or important as this one. We all have a yearning, a wound inside us, to leave a mark on the world when our time on earth is through. Mark shows us how to leave it where it matters most—in the foundation of the family tree. Like bright sun and a gentle rain on the soil of our lives, Mark's words and insight gives us what we need to grow deeper and stronger roots in our own often-withering branches. This isn't just a book for grandparents with teenage grandchildren. It's filled with humble wisdom on how to finish well, no matter the race you've been running. Mark has been a treasure to my family and countless others, and God-willing, if I get the chance to be a grandparent, his example will be my guiding light."

–Rory Feek, songwriter and singer

"This guy knows what he's talking about."

**–Chuck Swindoll, pastor and founder
of Insight for Living Ministries**

"As a grandparent of fifteen grandchildren ages two to twenty-two, I could not have imagined how rewarding and fulfilling it is to get to participate in the spiritual, social, and emotional growth of our ever growing "small village." Man, I love this game! But I need all the help I can get for this major call of duty. If there is anyone who knows more about pouring into kids of all ages than Mark Gregston, I've yet to meet him. Mark's latest book on grandparenting will undoubtedly make your adventure more filled with savvy and effectiveness while bringing an increase of wisdom to your fruit harvest on your beloved family tree."

–Joe White, Kanakuk Kamp

"The skills Mark teaches in this book are skills every grandparent should learn. From listening strategies to learning gratefulness, Mark's focus remains on strengthening the bonds between grandparents and their grandchildren is simple, yet life-changing ways."

    –Alan Carter, director of the NBC hit TV show *The Voice*

Grandparenting
TEENS

Grandparenting
TEENS

LEAVING A LEGACY OF HOPE

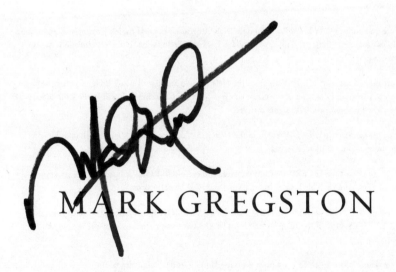

MARK GREGSTON

Forefront
BOOKS

DEDICATION

To Jan, my wife, and the greatest grandmother I know.

Who would have ever thought that a first date in ninth grade to see a Led

Zeppelin concert would one day lead to us being together fifty-one years later and

grandparents to four wonderful grandchildren: Maile, Macie, Chase, and Carter.

TABLE OF CONTENTS

Part IV:
Grandparents: Don't Save
What Is the Best for Last

Part V:
A Legacy They'll Never Forget

FOREWORD

*I*n this, his newest book, Mark Gregston addresses a huge vacuum in family help—grandparenting. For over forty years Mark and his wife, Jan, have been working with teenagers who are having a hard time navigating the rocky road of adolescence. As they state it, "Our goal is to restore what is broken, redeem what is lost, and defend the defenseless." They have helped an army of parents rescue their kids.

Few authors and counselors have addressed the issues of one of the greatest resources for rescuing and providing stability for kids at the most precarious junctures of their journeys—grandparents. Oh, there are books on how cute grandkids are and delightful books giving ideas for spending time with grandkids. But we grandparents need real, serious help solving knotty problems, tackling issues that threaten our families, and figuring out how to leave our grandchildren with deep convictions and strong character that instill principles for living in their own kids long after we are gone.

Early in 1990, Irene Endicott, a pioneer in the area of grand-parenting, went to the U.S. Census Bureau to find out how many grandparents there were in America. There were no such statistics. The question had never been asked on the census form. The closest was a question that asked a person what his/her relationship was to the others living in their home. Even AARP, the powerful national lobbying organization for older people, didn't know the number of grandparents in the United States.

Moreover, although many grandparents were raising their grand-kids because of dysfunction in the middle generation, they could not apply for or be granted foster parent status or subsidies, though many were supporting grandkids on limited incomes. Even at the publication of her first book *Grandparenting Redefined* in 1992, Endicott found that 5 percent of American families consisted of a grandparent raising a grandchild and that "one-third of initial child abuse calls received by children and youth agencies end[ed] with informal arrangements with relatives—mostly grandparents."[1]

Now, twenty-five years later, much has changed and not for the better. More families are in crisis, and more young people need grandparents than ever before.

The image of a gray-haired woman in a print dress and a man in bib overalls rocking on the porch is a long-gone fantasy. Most *grandmas* I know are zipping around on the mopeds they hauled to Florida on the back of their oversized motor homes. Even more, grandparents are themselves on the second and third marriages and share an assortment of step-grandchildren who don't remember a homeplace where they *can always go home to grandma.*

I'm just saying that grandkids and grandparents need real help and intelligent wisdom in these tumultuous days. How do we help without hovering? How do we enfold without enabling? How do we stay involved without intimidating? And how do we leave our kids and grandkids a legacy that *will not rust* and *where thieves cannot break in and steal?* How can we instill in the generations that follow a hunger for soul food that satisfies an unquenchable thirst for Living Water?

Bless Mark Gregston for wading into the deep waters of need with his pants legs rolled up and his sleeves too! Bless him for taking on us grandparents and our misconceptions of modern teenagers and for helping us see these kids with more potential and dearer hearts than we ever dreamed. And bless him for giving us the confidence to know that we can make an eternal difference in these less-than-optimistic times.

~Bill and Gloria Gaither

— PART I —

THEY LOVE
YOU WHEN
YOU'RE THERE

Chapter 1

EVEN WHEN YOU'RE OLDER THAN DIRT

I didn't know my grandparents. They were distant and old, like where they lived. One pair had settled in the small-town flatlands of Ryan, Oklahoma. It has a population of 6,000. And the other took up residence in the Kansas town of Concordia on the windswept plains in the middle of nowhere. Get the picture? By the time I was twelve, all my grandparents were in bad shape. They didn't seem to care much about my brother, my sister, or me.

I knew my dad's dad as one who was in and out of a nursing home. I remember watching him take out his teeth at dinner and eat bread that was soaked in milk. I don't remember him ever saying a word to me. There was never a connection between us.

My dad's mom was a quiet lady. She never said much of anything, but she laughed a lot. She traveled into the Oklahoma Territory in a covered wagon and lived in a log cabin in her adolescent years. Her dad had a huge mustache. She was not much for conversation, but she loved to make chocolate cake. Every time I see a chocolate cake, I think of her chocolate cake—but not much else.

The only thing I can remember about my mom's dad are his views of anyone who wasn't white, and let's just say his views don't bear repeating. He also didn't have time for us, so we never made time for him.

My mom's mom was frail and somewhat critical in spirit. I never saw her laugh, never enjoyed being with her and my grandpa, and couldn't wait to drive away from that little north Kansas town whenever we were there.

You now know the total of all my memories of my grandparents. Isn't that sad? In just five short paragraphs, you know everything about the roles my grandparents played in my life (or didn't play, which is more like it). It's not that I hated them. I just wasn't sure I loved them, as it's hard to love someone with whom you have no relationship. There were no values or morals transferred. There were no stories of family traditions of fun times together. Never a mention of what they believed or hoped for. No instruction. No wisdom shared. And, sadly, no love lost when each passed away.

I grew up with the notion that grandparents were people you saw occasionally, who retired at sixty-five, and were dead by seventy, people who exerted little or no influence on their grandkids or made any real impact on them. I am determined to be a different kind of grandparent than that.

WHEN A RELATIONSHIP CAN GROW

So when my daughter told me when I was forty-six that I was going to be a grandfather, it scared me to death. I had no idea what I was supposed to do or what this grandparenting thing was supposed to look like. My examples were negative and unlike the kind of grandparent I wanted to be.

But I was excited. Deep down, I knew a new adventure was about to unfold. I couldn't wait.

My first thought upon hearing, "You're going to be a grandpa!" was, *I can't be that old.* I was somewhat hesitant to admit to others that I was going to become one. I never thought the young lady I started dating in the ninth grade and married six years later would end up being a grandparent with me. Did that mean I was going to be sleeping with a *grandma* the rest of my days? The whole concept of this new role petrified me. I even remember telling my daughter, "I'm probably not going to do well with this grandchild until they reach their teens . . . so don't expect much."

When the day came, I waited outside my daughter's birthing room and I wondered what this grandpa thing was going to be. Then I heard this little six-pound, eight-ounce newborn cry seconds after my granddaughter was born, and my life changed forever. It was a heart change that mellowed this type-A personality into a pup. I couldn't quit crying. I couldn't take enough photographs.

The first time I actually held my granddaughter, I wondered if my grandparents ever held me when I was born. I wondered if they felt the same thing the first time they saw me. I don't think they did. I determined right then to *do it differently.* I wanted to have a relationship with my grandkids. I did not want to be remembered as someone who ate milk-soaked bread and never spoke, one who made racist comments, one who was critical all the time, or one who just made a great chocolate cake.

I wanted, and still want, to leave a legacy—something that makes a profound difference in the lives of my grandkids. I want to influence them in the best possible ways, ways I know that only I can. Of all the grandparents and all the grandkids in the world, mine were chosen for me. I take that seriously. It is an honor and a privilege. I want to leave them a legacy of hope.

If that legacy is to be, you have to work at the relationship continually. I knew that I would have to experiment with new ways of connecting rather than those I observed in my years of being a grandchild. And I knew that if I wanted to remain a part of their lives beyond their preteen years, I was going to have to make that happen.

I believe this: God (with the help of medicine) is keeping you around a little longer so you can have influence, impact, and a make a marked impression on the lives of your grandkids. That's the legacy I mentioned earlier.

If you're going to be involved in the lives of your grandchildren and desperately want to make a mark on their lives, then that relationship needs to be active and *up to date*. You have to understand their world for the words, guidance, and wisdom you'll need. You have to change with the times. You have to make adjustments. Pursue their hearts on their terms. Learn to bite your tongue. Determine when to speak, and when *not* to, and when you have enough of their attention so they can feel a sense of rest with just you.

I know because I've spent the last forty years watching grandparents get involved in the lives of their grandkids. We have had over three thousand kids live us through the years at Heartlight, our residential counseling center for struggling teens. I've seen the impact many grandparents have had, and an equal number of *failures to connect* from other grandparents. Certain traits connect grandkids to grandparents, and there are behaviors that prevent positive, impactful relationships from ever happening.

Your grandkids need you now more than ever, especially in their teen years. God has a plan to use you as a messenger of timeless truth in their ever-changing world. Your position is unique. Your relationship is paramount. Pursue it well. Make the most of the years you have to invest in the lives of your grandkids. Be a message of truth in their ever-changing world.

THEY'LL CHOOSE YOU IF YOU CHOOSE THEM

It was a hot, humid day in East Texas—one of those burning, scorching days where Texans wish they were somewhere a thousand miles north of where they live. It was so hot that the only places to battle the heat were inside with the air conditioning cranked up, outside in the swimming pool, or playing in the sprinkler in your front yard.

Maile, my first granddaughter, chose the new, turtle-shaped sprinkler. She was nineteen months old and spending the day with Mamaw (my wife, Jan). The heat lingered on this Texas afternoon.

I was driving home from work and turned into our driveway, a hundred-yard road that leads to our home. As soon as I pulled in, I could see Jan in the front yard. The turtle sprayed cool water. Maile stood in the front yard butt naked, laughing and jumping through the spraying fountain of water.

As I drove up, Maile spotted me and immediately sprinted toward me. Seeing her, I stopped my truck and got out to hear her screaming excitedly at the top of her lungs, "Poppa! Poppa!" Her little arms were waving, and her legs ran toward me as fast as they could.

I stood there and all of a sudden, everything went into slow motion. My brain wanted to stop and take it all in. My heart just wanted to savor the moment. The innocence of that simple moment, watching this tiny little girl in nothing but her shoes, so excited to see her Poppa, immediately brought tears to my eyes and such joy to my heart. I laughed and cried at the same time. And I knew . . . I mean, I *knew* from the bottom of my heart that I had a place in hers.

She jumped into my arms. I stood there, holding this soaking wet, twenty-pound little girl as she hugged my neck, begging me to play in the sprinkler with her. Later Jan told me she had never seen me smile as big as I did that day. I joked with my wife that she would see me smile like that more often if she greeted me like Maile did every time I arrived home.

That day revealed how special my relationship with my granddaughter was, and continues to be, as is my relationship with all my grandchildren. I promised myself I would do the work necessary to keep it going.

That promise was pretty easy to keep the first twelve years of Maile's life. During that period, I could do no wrong. When your kids first have kids, you *ooh* and *ahh* over that new baby and bring on the gifts. The sheer cuteness factor of the child keeps grandparents attached and connected. Matter of fact, grandparents might even score a coffee mug that says, "World's Greatest Grandpa" (or "Grandma"), or a T-shirt that states, "Grandpa: the Man, the Myth, the Legend" or "SuperGrandma" during your grandkids' elementary school years.

Once Maile reached middle school, keeping our relationship special became harder. The competition for time with her increased, and I realized if I didn't remain a part of her life, the bond I'd committed to maintaining would soon be a casualty of adolescent interests taking her to *greener pastures*.

As your grandkids get a little older, their social circles grow as well. The amount of time they have for you becomes scarcer. As they enter their teen years, time with grandparents gets pushed to the side. Other interests take your place during your grandchildren's teen years.

Before you know it, they're off to college, and the distance in space and time grows even larger. Then they get married, and the time slot once reserved for grandparents shrinks more. Once your grandchildren have kids, just about the only time your grandchildren see our *crown of old men* is on holidays, in an occasional album photograph, or on Facebook. If they still use a phone, we might get a quick catch-up cell call.

I'm sure you've attended many funerals of grandparents where the only mention of interactions with the grandkids were those that took place during their preteen years. It's the "busyness" of a teen's schedule that tends to eliminate those grandparents who aren't intentional and calculated about their involvement in the lives of their teen grandchildren.

It's important to remember your role in their lives is still vital. You have to make it happen. You have to be the one who pursues the relationships during their teen years because of their calendars and crunch times, which are the beginning of the *great divide*. It's hard to recover real relationship in your later years.

Amid all the choices your grandkids have in their lives, you can help them make spending time with you an easy decision. Because they sense your love for them that has been demonstrated through your active pursuit of a relationship with them.

So make it an easy choice.

MAINTAIN IT

That's really what this book is all about. Understanding the world your grandkids live in and figuring out how to be part of it. Period. Their world is different from the one we grew up in. A grandparent's greatest challenge is to determine how to remain relevant and needed, just as you did in the early stages of this special relationship that changed your world the moment they entered it

While you might have been quite active in your grandkid's lives when they were preteens, a whole new strategy of involvement has got to be determined if you want to continue that beneficial involvement during their adolescent years when they need you the most. Just as their lives are changing, so must you. You can't keep correcting their mistakes. You're going to have to accept some things in their lives that weren't acceptable in yours. Your communication style has got to change as they mature and need to hear a different message that pertains to *their* stage in life.

It was easy for me to quote scripture, share stories, and tell jokes to my grandchildren during their preteen years. They listened to every word I had to say. Whatever we did, they loved because Poppa was spending time with them. Then they became teens and distractions started to pull their attention in other directions. As my grandkids' lives become more complicated and serious, my role leaned more toward sharing wisdom about dating, boyfriend breakups, and exposure to a whole new world they were entering. I helped them find answers to the questions they were asking. And then my grandparenting style had to shift when they reached their adolescent years.

You've got to allow your grandkids to become young men and women, to become husbands and wives, and eventually, moms and dads. Lord willing, one day they'll even be grandmas and grandpas. And your legacy can continue through them into their own grandchildren.

There is a great need for a connection with you when they don't even recognize it. They may be faced with new challenges so you must resolve to transform your grandparenting style to continue to be where you are a safe place, a place where you listen more than you speak, encourage more than you correct, and laugh more often with them than you become upset by their actions.

Don't think a yearly vacation together is enough to keep the relational fires burning between you and your grandchild any more than a once-a-year connection with friends maintains real relationships. It's not where you vacation, it's how you get there that makes the difference. Kind words, interest in their world, asking what they think, and humble offers to help any way you can all year-long make that annual vacation a memory builder and unforgettable experience.

Here's my point: You've got to make the relationship happen.

THEY'RE GROWING UP

Your grandchild is busy growing up, becoming social, maturing, and trying out independence in their teen years. All that growth and maturity try to push grandparents right out of the picture. Don't let it.

You have a choice to make. You can allow the relationship to fade or take the role God has placed before you. All grandparents can have a positive influence on kids even in a day and age where influential relationships are in short supply and low demand. It's not as much about what you do as it is creating an atmosphere where relationships can grow. It's about adapting to their world where they can learn more about who you are.

Here's another piece of advice: Do it now. Time is flying by and we'll be gone before we know it.

I don't want to go and have my kids or grandkids shed tears over a sense of regret that Momma and Poppa *weren't* involved in the life of his family. I want them to cry tears of joy that Momma and Poppa *have been involved* in every stage of their lives.

Chapter 2

WHY GRAY HAIR IS AN ADVANTAGE

The glory of young men is their strength,

but the splendor of old men is their gray hair.

Proverbs 20:29 (ESV)

W hat do your grandkids call you?
  Soon-to-be grandparents wrangle over what they want to be called. I tell them it doesn't matter what the kids call you; you'll love whatever name they attach to you.

I've heard some crazy ones just to prove my point. And grandparents like them.

Busoma, BooBoo, Oompa, Suggy, Bop-Bop, Botchie, Amma, GaGa, Bearbsie, Poppa Bear, Bla-Bla (now, that's an interesting one), Birdie, Big Grandpa, Bomp, and, of course, Bobaloo.

Call grandparents whatever you want. Make fun of all the various nicknames but when a child calls you by a special name, a grandparent feels wanted and needed.

My grandkids call me *Poppa* in front of me. I'm sure they say other things behind my back. But *Poppa* pretty much gets my full attention. Once when I was in Moscow, Russia, a young girl ran up to me and said, "Poppa!" Evidently, that's a common word for fathers in Russia, and she immediately had my attention. She then said, "Take me!" She said only three words, but because she said, "Poppa," she had my immediate attention. I felt I should do whatever she said. I even called Jan and told her we should adopt her. There's something special that happens when you hear the name you were given by a grandchild.

I must say I spoil my grandkids. I give them just about anything they want. It's what grandparents are supposed to do. When they want to go somewhere, want something special, and *need* something, I'm pretty much a sucker for helping any way I can.

As they get older, I want to keep that same position in their lives. I want to connect when they're going somewhere, wanting something, and needing more, which can't be satisfied by the expenditure of cash but by sharing wisdom and counsel.

Please hear once again that my intent isn't to circumvent or go around the parents as if to somehow hold a higher position in a child's life.

My intent is to be a helpmate to my kids and to support and encourage their desires for their kids. A voice from outside the home (a grandparent's voice) can affirm and support, as well as uphold rules, expectations, and the desires of the parents in the lives of grandkids. I want to help my kids and grandkids by giving a different perspective that still ends up at the same place. It just starts from a different spot.

Maybe it's the gray hair that attracts kids to me. Or maybe it's the mustache I wear in the style of the 1880s that reassures them they're talking to an old guy who might just have some answers. I want to think I've earned every one of my gray hairs. I'm proud of them even though when they began showing up on my head, I plucked them out as it embarrassed me to be getting older.

Proverbs 16:31 (NRSV) affirms my love of my gray hair: "Gray hair is a crown of glory; it is gained in a righteous life."

Darn right, it is. And I'm going to use it any way I can to benefit those around me.

THE HUNT'S ON FOR WISDOM

When I was a Young Life leader (Young Life is a worldwide ministry to kids), I thought I would lose my effectiveness by age twenty-five. I thought maybe I would be too old by that age. Then as a youth minister, I thought my gig would be up at thirty when I crossed the age to be considered "over the hill." When kids came to live with Jan and me at Heartlight, I began to think, "Okay, by forty, kids will stop listening to me." In my forties, I thought the half-century mark would close down the stream of teens coming to me to talk. Then I turned fifty, and one day as I was plucking out gray hairs, it occurred to me I was no longer a *young thang* with whom kids wanted to talk. I was a guy who was showing his age and teens actually wanted more.

Now that I'm sixty, I've come to realize that age and a little gray hair are magnets to teens who want wisdom. Now I'm working hard to keep all this gray stuff I have. I've put away the tweezers and feel pretty comfortable with this aging process. It affords me a different spot in the lives of my grandkids they can get from no one else.

They're searching for wisdom. What they are getting from their peers, television, and the internet is an overwhelming flow of information that doesn't always have substance. It's easy to find information, but not context or truth. Whether it's Siri or Alexa, anyone can tell you what time it is or help you order a pizza. They can't help you ponder the meaning of life or how a relationship works. I want to give them what they can't find anywhere else—wisdom that takes into account the faults, struggles, makeup, genetics, history, tradition, and difficulties within this thing called *family*. Wisdom shared with perspective.

Wisdom is so much more than a collection of great comments. Teens have already heard it all. What they desire is for the "word to become flesh" (see John 1:14) and to see the application of all they have been taught through their preteen years. It's basically a plea of, "Don't tell me. Show me. Give me an example to follow, not just words to live by."

Granddad, or whatever name you go by, don't worry you're not saying the right thing. Many men feel inadequate if they lack wise words to share at the right time. That's okay. Your teen grandkids aren't buying the words they hear anymore; they want to see those words in action.

Grandmas, or if your grandkids call you Amma or Bop-Bop, it's not about your words once they reach the teen years. Quit talking so much and start showing them how your words line up with your actions. Talk less. Show more.

ENTER WISDOM

These are the ways teens pick up wisdom.

Observation
First, they're watching you. In their quietness and cognitive processing, your grandkids are seeing whether your actions support the words you say. Is the truth out there in real life?

You're being watched. They watch how you interact with other drivers, waitresses, flight attendants, fellow workers, employees, landscapers, and those you do business with. They are watching how to speak to your spouse, how you treat your dog, and how you handle conflict. They observe how much you laugh, how much you cry, and how much you hurt. They take notice at what you look at, what you read, and how you care for folks who have less than you. And they learn from how you treat other kids and how you act toward those who hurt you. They are watching how you live out the wisdom you have shared with them.

They are processing traits such as forgiveness, grace, love, empathy, sympathy, encouragement, boldness, and integrity by comparing what they see vs. what they've been taught for so many years.

In order to see and observe, it's imperative that time is spent together. One can't see what isn't there.

Reflection

When your grandkids leave your presence, what do they think about? Do you leave them thinking about anything?

Reflection happens when a grandchild considers what you said or what they saw in your actions. Sometimes you may leave them with a question rather than always giving them the answers. Or it may be a statement given, not to show what a gray-headed stud you are, but to provoke their thinking.

Look, I believe most of your grandkids have grown up in a world where the seeds of truth have been scattered throughout their lives. When they reach their teen years, we need to scale back planting and spend more time cultivating. Cultivation includes turning the soil, adding fertilizer, watering, providing light, and sometimes pulling weeds. Cultivation can move them out of dormancy into productivity.

Encouraging reflection is a way of engaging your grandchildren to take responsibility for their thinking and process life in a way that moves them on to emotional and spiritual maturity.

Try this: The next time you see one of your grandkids, find a quiet time to share with them. Tell them, "There's nothing you can do to make me love you more, and there's nothing you can do to make me love you less." It's a powerful statement that lets them know of your undying love for them, and it also gets them to think about your relationship. Teens know people love them when they're doing well; I'm not sure they believe that to be true when they're not.

Shift the way you mesh with your grandkids, and you'll shift their desire from wanting just dollars from you to wanting more, something they can't get anywhere else.

Experience

I used to think if I didn't pray at the table before a meal or have a devotion at some opportune time or say something spiritual at the right moment, my kids or grandkids would never get to see the deep love I have for God or experience the joy I have because of a relationship with Him. I don't think that anymore.

The emotions of a lifetime are often found in the all-but-forgotten experiences of adolescence.

I believe as we hide God's Word in our heart, memorize His truth, and internalize His love for us, the expression of Him comes out at the most unexpected times. It sometimes comes out in the form of laughter. Or is articulated in a discussion that doesn't fall back on *Christianese* but is principled on truth. It can be communicated through conversations that toss in golden nuggets of truth and wisdom that can only come from God himself. Or it can be uttered in the most amazing and surprising locations and situations where we least expect it.

At this point, your actions speak louder than your words. As you experience travel, meals, special occasions, vacations, funerals, weddings, and plenty of normal interactions, God will allow His Word to become flesh through you.

Spend more time lining up experiences than giving things that are one day going to rot, get destroyed, or become outdated. Buy a boat or a WaveRunner. Get that house at the lake. Try a new grill for your patio and grill meals they'll never forget. Go on a hunting trip. Take a trip to New York with your granddaughters. Go to concerts. Attend the Country Music Awards. Take a trip to the Grand Canyon. Plan things that include your grandkids.

I owned a Harley and realized it was something my grandkids couldn't do with me. They weren't going to get on the back and go for a ride with me and every time I rode, I rarely saw any other biker toting along their grandkids. What I noticed was that every time I got on the bike, I felt guilty about not spending time where it could have been better invested in the lives of my family members.

I see grandparents purchasing RVs and leaving their family behind to travel the country. I see other grandparents retiring and moving to where they can do what they've always wanted to do. They take up hobbies that don't include the grandkids. There's nothing wrong with any of these, but I would encourage you to plan and create experiences often with your grandchildren. They should know their grandparents aren't just people who have fun but are people who are fun to be with because of the shared experiences grandparents and grandchildren enjoy together.

Wisdom can be found in the lives of grandparents who have a wealth of insight and understanding. But it can only be imparted if those grandparents create an environment for their grandkids to discover that wisdom in them.

Chapter 3

YOU CAN CHANGE GEARS WHEN THEY THINK YOU'RE OUT OF GAS

From everyone who has been given much, much will be

demanded; and from the one who has been entrusted

with much, much more will be asked.

<small>LUKE 12:48 (NIV)</small>

*I*t's time to change gears. Shift those gears before you run out of gas. Even if your gears are rusty, you can't get stuck in neutral, drive, or reverse and be a truly successful grandparent. You have to shift gears at the right times to meet the changing needs of your grandkids and their parents. In the teen years, you even have to get out of the car and let your grandkids take a turn at the wheel.

For now, do you remember what you read earlier about how grandparents need to shift their style of grandparenting and *change gears* to accommodate the needs of their children's children? The time is now when they become teens. If grandparents don't shift, then the only stories shared as people remember your legacy will be those that occurred when they were grandkids.

If you don't switch your grandparenting style from the way you parented or were parented, you'll be out of touch, as antiquated as your grandmother's sewing machine. You may be accused of never letting those special kids grow into the people God destined them to be. Nor will you get to have any of the deep discussions that will sprout from all the hard-earned wisdom you attained.

The first twelve years of your grandkids' lives are a time of teaching. A time where parents pour into their kids and allow them to be involved in everything the Christian world has to offer. It's a time of planting seeds and imparting the need to follow the biblical principles that parents hold dear to their heart.

It's the parents' responsibility to plant these seeds of faith, not the grandparents (unless the grandparents are raising the grandkids). Some grandparents don't feel like the parents are instilling enough of a Christian lifestyle into the hearts of the grandkids, so the grandparents must intervene to make up the difference between so-so and great teaching.

Without knowing better, the grandparents' cards and texts are interpreted more like judgment rather than encouragement. The grandparents' role during the teen years is to cultivate the soil to hold the seeds planted through the parents' efforts in a grandchild's earlier years. When grandparents try to teach when what is needed is training, everyone gets frustrated.

You have a role in the lives of your grandkids. If you want to fulfill that role to the fullest during their teen years, be the one who helps in the training process. Take what has been taught and help them apply truth to their lives. Be as effective as you can in fulfilling the role that is greatly lacking and significantly needed in their lives. There's no one else who can do this as well as you because of the position God has placed you in.

MOVING YOUR KIDS FROM IMMATURITY TO WHO THEY CAN BE

When your grandchildren enter their teen years, you must switch your model of influence from teaching to training. Let me break it down into lists of what you need and will really want to do.

Showing What Maturity Looks Like

Twelve-year-olds are expected to be immature. They are. As they turn thirteen, it's important that everyone involved in the life of the child begin the push to maturity. Grandparents are no exception. A grandparent's home is not to be a place where a young thirteen- to fourteen-year-old can retreat and escape the growing-up process. That would be in direct conflict with the desires of the parents.

No one wants to have a twenty-five-year-old clown hanging out on the sofa playing video games with no job, no drive, and no direction in life. I hope you didn't let your kids do that. Or your grandparents didn't let *you* do it either. Once kids enter the teen years, it's time to start growing up.

Encouraging maturity includes, but is not limited to, all the following items I've listed. The real challenge in this changing of the gears is in the mindsets of the parents and grandparents. Instead of looking at your child (or grandchild) as this neat little kid and enjoying every part of him or her, the focus should be on a time of preparation for what you want to see in the future.

It is shifting gears from a teaching model to a training model. Teaching is the gear all should be engaged in the first twelve years. Training is the next gear. And it's not an automatic. It will not happen on its own. It's a determined conviction on the part of parents and grandparents to help children take what they have been taught and put it into play in their life. Then they can mature and develop out of a self-centered, entitled mindset where they wake up in the morning and ask, "What's everyone going to do for me today?"

Moving Them from Dependence on You to Developing Independence

Children are dependent on their parents and grandparents for everything. If the goal is to help your grandchildren develop a healthy independence by the time they reach the age of eighteen, then the training has to happen now as they leave childhood behind. Teaching gives them the tools; training allows them to use them.

Chances are, everyone has been doing pretty much everything for your grandchild up to this point. Someone has made all their decisions and taken responsibilities for every area of their life. They've had total control of behavior, given them all the answers, and lectured them until they're blue in the face. If you don't switch gears, you'll end up with that twenty-five-year-old I referred to.

Here are some examples that might help you understand this a little better. If a child is taught about school, the need to do homework, and get good grades, then at some point the child must be allowed to determine when to study, hand in their own work, and even take the risk of failing. If and when they experience failure, they begin to learn that no one else is going to do the work for them.

It's funny to have all the parents and grandparents at the science fair laugh about how much work they put into their fourth graders' science projects. Parents and grandparents come up with a good idea, do all the work, and pretty much oversee the whole project. But it's not that funny when the kids hit ninth grade. It's sad. The problem is not the child. It's the parents and grandparents encouraging immaturity.

Parents and grandparents tell grandchildren from the age of one to twelve what to do. When you begin to switch to the training model, you move from telling them what they must do to asking, "What do you think you ought to do?"

Posing the question to the children means they'll have to dig through their memory banks and pull out the file of what they were taught to do in that kind of situation. This is where parents and grandparents allow the child to begin to think critically. Everyone's always done it for them; it's now their turn before others continue to do it for them.

You grandparents or parents, pass the ball to them. Will they stumble? Sure they will. Just like you did the first time you were given a chance to run with the ball. If they do stumble, they'll get back up because you shifted gears from being a teacher and moved into the role of trainer. As the trainer on the sidelines, you encourage them to brush off their knees and keep going.

Move from Your Decisions to Helping Them
Learn to Make Their Decisions

Decision-making is important. If you want your grandchild to be able to make big and important decisions later in life, you've got to give them the opportunity to flex their decision-making muscles. The more they work out now, the better shape they'll be in when they are truly out on their own. Is it easier, more time-saving, and far more convenient to keep making the decisions ourselves? Absolutely. Does it stunt the growth of our grandkids' maturity? Absolutely.

Let them decide when they need to study for school. Now, if you have a child who can't stop playing video games or gets consumed with chatting or texting friends, then, sure, you've got to intervene. Where there are no internal boundaries, grandparents (and parents) have to establish external boundaries.

By thirteen years of age, they need to decide what they are going to wear to school. Next is whether they're going to brush their teeth, wear sunscreen at the beach, or purchase new clothes.

It's easier to let them go on and depend on you. They can blame you for bad outcomes of their decisions. You and I know transferring the responsibility to make good decisions is a process. It will take time but is well worth the effort.

Let them begin to decide where to eat dinner. What TV programs to watch. What time to go to bed. What music to listen to. Whether or not they play sports. At some point, which church they go to or whether they go at all. Who they're going to date. Whether they need a job. How they spend their Saturdays. Who their friends are.

Remember that the goal here is allowing them to flex those decision-making muscles while you're still around to ultimately help lift the weight off their chest if it falls. Then there is still time to have those deeper discussions about what happened when they made a mistake or a not-so-good choice and what they could do better next time.

I'm not encouraging you as a grandparent to allow every decision to be made by your grandchild. There have got to be some home rules in place, so a grandchild knows that some decisions have already been made for them. Yes, you do want your home to be a place of rest for your grandkids, but you don't want it to be a place that is out of control where they get to do anything and everything they want. Rules without relationship may cause rebellion. Relationships without rules cause chaos.

Move from You Doing It to Them Doing It

Quit doing everything for them. Revolving our lives around our kids and grandkids is easy. But if entitlement and selfishness run rampant in a culture that is *all about me,* then you are the ones to break that cycle. If you don't, then you will have an irresponsible and immature selfish teen on your hands who enters their twenties about to head into disaster. Their health may take a beating, lives may derail, or marriages may fail.

In an effort to help kids understand I'm not their servant, maid, tutor, slave, or employee, I tell them, "I owe you nothing, but I want to give you everything. Still, I owe you nothing." I want them to be responsible for their own lives and break the habit of selfishness supported by their *culture of me.*

So when I choose to do something for them or give them anything, it's not because I have to. It's because I want to. I want them to know that my actions are not something that they are entitled to, but hopefully, now, feel a sense of gratefulness that I have done something for them. It's how I position my longing to provide for them and a concept that can change their future relationships.

In the teen years, it's time for them to start doing their own laundry. Let them pack for their own vacation. Let them choose their own hairstyle. Let them purchase their own clothes, no matter how awful they look. Let them put their own gas in the car. Let them learn how to use an alarm clock now, so you don't have eighteen-year-olds in college who can't get out of bed. Let them be responsible for their own academics and let them take their own clothes to the cleaners.

Quit doing everything for them.

Move from Your Control to Their Control

Give teens control. Changing gears and letting them start to control, that's what's going to happen anyway. It's already happened by age thirteen. It's much more effective and relationship-building to let go of the wheel.

Attempts to take control from them may prevent them from learning self-control. You want them to be in control. Don't you? I do! I want my grandchildren to have control when they get pulled over by a policeman for speeding. I want them to have control with a girlfriend or boyfriend. I want them to learn restraint with their words when they're provoked. I want them to take control of their academic pursuits. I want them to learn how to use their money so they can become financially responsible. I want them to embrace the concept of keeping their mouths shut when it would be easier to fire off comments that will only cause more damage.

I tell the kids who live with us that I really don't care whether they pass or flunk their classes at our school. Isn't that a great thing to say to students, coming from a founder of a boarding school? Truth be told, I do care. But I don't accept responsibility for their academics. I tell them they have control and can make the decision to complete high school whenever they want. It is my way of giving up control and giving it to them, in hopes that they'll learn that their life is about them, not about me.

SHOWING THEM HOW TO LISTEN

Move from Giving Answers to Asking Questions

As grandparents, we always have a comment, an answer, or the right way of doing things. We'll be way better off with my decision. There's some truth there. But when we know everything there's no room for their search for answers.

Quit being the answer man or answer woman. Begin to let your grandkids do some searching on their own. If they don't learn it now, they'll only have to learn it when they're apart from us.

Let them ask questions. Your conversations should contain phrases such as the following:

What do you think we should do about you driving drunk?

What would you do if you were lied to like your friend?

What do you think would be the best alternative to resolve the conflict between you and your dad?

Did you think that was fair for you to get caught cheating and others didn't?

Would you have done the same thing if you were in her shoes?

What do you think is the greatest struggle teens face today?

What do you think about the legalization of marijuana?

Do you think politics are as messy as they seem?

When your grandchildren answer, hold your tongue and don't correct them. Keep yourself from telling them where they are wrong. If they ask you what you think, even then you should not always answer. Many times your answer will stop the conversation (because you probably just shared the best answer. What else can your grandchild add at that point?). If you want them to come to the right answer themselves, let them figure it out.

Please beware of this: no manipulation. Don't ask questions so that you can listen to what they have to say and gain a platform to share your opinion. This is what I call *selfish questioning* because it's not really about your grandchild. It's more about your need to talk.

Always ask questions. Quit giving the answers.

Move from Lecturing to Having Discussions

This one is easy. Move from all those lectures that you realize are producing nothing and begin to have discussions full of opinions, questions, differing thoughts, and controversial stances. Often you will not be able to solve any of the world's problems. And even if you think you can, it's wise to keep the solution to yourself and see if your grandchildren can come to the same conclusion by themselves.

Remember, you want to keep the conversation going. Your goal is to be a place of wisdom your grandchild can visit over and over again.

Move from Telling to a Model of Sharing

Along the same vein of having discussions, movement from the teaching to the training model means a shift in the way you reveal what you have to say. It can no longer be, "This is the way it is. Period." It's got to be more of a, "This is what I think," or, "This is what I believe."

Many times I ask teens if they want a response from me. I ask, "Do you want an answer or my opinion?" Sometimes they say, "Neither." I leave it at that. Successful grandparents know it creates a safe place for teens to hash out what they're trying to work through. It also leaves the door open for them to come back.

Move from Talking to Listening

Here's another tough one. The times when you used to just talk to your grandkids need to be replaced with spending more time listening once they enter their teen years. Many times kids tell me that the ol' grandfolks just like to hear themselves talk and never listen to what the teen wants to say.

As one grandparent to another, you've had your time to talk. Now it is your time to listen.

How would you rather be known? As one who talked all the time or one who was a great listener? Wise grandparents desire the latter.

Listen.

LEARNING WHAT IT MEANS TO GROW UP

Punishment used to be easy to dole out when your grandchildren were little—violate the home policy, get into trouble. It was all about following your rules, doing what you said, without question. Punishment steered them away from wrong choices. It gave them understanding that good choices bring pleasure and foolish choices bring pain. Punishment kept foolish choices from happening (or at least nipped them in the bud). But punishment changes as it moves into an older group of kids, that is, teens.

Move from Punishment to Their Understanding of the Value in Discipline

Now you're moving away from punishment into a world of discipline. Discipline now helps a child choose where they want to go and keeps them from ending up in a place they don't want to be. It's not about the infliction of pain. It emphasizes making good decisions. Discipline lets adolescents and teens know you're working with them in their choices to help, not to force them to do or not do things.

When teens know you're working with them and want to help get them to a better place in life, they'll welcome the limits, restrictions, and boundaries set around them. When they believe you're just out to punish them, they push back hard against your limits.

Move from Your Responsibility to Encouraging Their Responsibility

As kids enter their teen years, the greatest gift a parent or grandparent can give is helping their children in the process of accepting making choices so they can learn to accept responsibility for their own lives. This, in turn, will produce emotional, spiritual, and relational maturity.

Maturity is a byproduct of responsibility. If anyone in the family prevents a child's acceptance of responsibility for his own life, then they are doing too much for that child, i.e., making too many decisions, keeping the control, and refusing to trust the child.

Remember the verse from the beginning of this chapter? Let's reread it. Luke 12:48 states something I believe is key to the training process:

From everyone who has been given much, much will be demanded; and from the one who has been entrusted with much, much more will be asked.

What I'm proposing in this training model is the transfer of quite a bit to your grandkids. While this means they'll experience more freedom in their pursuit of independence, it also means more will be required from them as well.

Move the Emphasis from What You Do to Who You Are

As kids move from concrete to abstract thinking in their teen years, it's important for grandparents to make a shift in their messages and discussions to be more about helping a teen understand that who they are is more important than what they do. When you are doing, it has more to do with behavior. When you shift to showing who you are, you reveal your character. Many times grandparents are more concerned about the everyday, surface behavior they see and experience rather than working on the heart and building their grandchildren's character. Grandparents can hone in on those occasional momentary glimpses of greatness and help their grandkids see it in themselves too.

Grandparents help grandchildren understand that their greatness may feel locked inside for now but will soon be revealed in who they become. It's a message of hope and promise that can only come from a grandparent who is more concerned about where they are headed than where they have been.

As a final word about shifting your style of grandparenting from teaching to training, let me share this: If parents make this transition and grandparents don't, then Grandpa and Grandma will be ignored and placed on the shelf. Along with their shelving will be all the great wisdom and insight they possess. Kids want to grow up. They want to take responsibility for their lives. They want to make decisions. They want to be mature. They want to be in control. That "want" needs to be coupled with an example of how to accomplish all those desires. That example is you. And they need to hear your wisdom as to how they will always side with those who help them move toward independence and resist those who impede their progress.

Make sure they side with you. Move over to the passenger side and hand over the keys of decision-making before you run out of gas. It may be a wild ride, but the journey is thrilling and the destination well worth the price!

Chapter 4

MAINTAINING YOUR RELATIONSHIP IN A NOT-SO-RELATIONAL CULTURE

Therefore let us not pass judgment on one another any

longer, but rather decide never to put a stumbling

block or hindrance in the way of a brother.

ROMANS 14:13 (ESV)

I really feel that grandkids are a reward for not killing your own kids. I'm joking. I'm joking. I love my kids.

My daughter recently looked at me and said, "Dad, it's almost as if you like them more than us." I replied with a smirk on my face and a little bit of truth in my tone, "Is it that evident?"

There is something very, very special about a relationship with your grandchildren. There is no other relationship quite like it. When I am a great-grandparent, and my daughter is a grandparent, I am sure she will understand.

As I watch my grandkids grow and change, the type of relationship I have with them changes too. The reason for the change? So I can maintain the relationship that began the day these grandkids were born.

Your grandkids need good, lasting, committed relationships that don't stop when they don't respond. They need strong grandparent ties that weather the every-other-week stormy times of adolescence. They especially need a deep relationship with their grandparents because they're not getting those relational needs filled by their peers—at least not in wise, healthy ways. Our grandkids and their friends spend most of their time in the shallow end of the relationship pool, never venturing into the deeper water of commitment and genuineness.

MY PARENTS AND GRANDPARENTS DEMAND PERFECTION

Because of the need in all of us to know and be known, it's essential you spend time reflecting on your own life and the impact you can have on your grandkids. You must continually review the things in your life that may push them away. Look at the log in your own eye rather than the speck in the eye of your grandchild. You'll never be able to address the speck if the log is blocking your vision. Nor will they let you.

I've found there are some ways of engaging with teens that shut kids down and push them away. For grandparents, these can ruin relationships.

I've never heard a mother say, "I want to have a perfect daughter." I've never heard a dad say, "I'm going to rule my home with an iron fist. It's either my way or the highway." I've never heard a mom and dad say, "We want to be judgmental parents."

But I have heard hundreds of young ladies say, "My mom wants me to be perfect." I've heard hundreds of young men say, "My dad is so strong-headed I can't wait to get out of the house." I've heard thousands of kids say, "My parents are the most judgmental people I know."

This applies to grandparents as well. Because parents pick up these styles from one place. From their own parents, most likely. Yes, from you.

Where does the disconnect come from? Parents and grandparents long to be loving, forgiving, and grace-filled. Kids often see them as critical, negative, and strict, so who's right and who's wrong? Or is it really a matter of right and wrong at all? Aren't we all on the same team?

Let me explain the common complaints I hear from teens.

Perfection—what we Christians call *excellence*—is easy to ask of grandkids in their early years. Christ was a model of perfection (see Hebrews 10:14). Most young kids really believe the world is ideal, they are awesome, and their parents are textbook picture-perfect. As they enter adolescence, all that falls right off the pedestal. So do their parents and grandparents. Their eyes are opened to a world that isn't great and perfect like they'd been told. And disillusionment sets in.

One of the major changes in a child moving into adolescence is the switching of their minds from concrete to abstract thinking. Their perception of the world increases, and their concept of perfection changes as they get zits, hair, and other grown-up parts. They get made fun of, experience rejection and disappointment, question their existence, and don't feel like they belong.

Many times encouragement from adults now feels like a demand for perfection. They take questions about grades as insults for not making all As. They interpret comments about weight or the need to watch what you eat as you saying they are fat. They hear remarks about being on the cell phone all the time that imply, or outright state, that they are rude. When they lash out in frustration, it is often misdiagnosed as disrespect when they really don't mean to be disrespectful.

At the beginning of the adolescent years, teens and 'tweens (early adolescence kids) are fragile and sensitive. They can appear ambivalent, unsure, uncertain, indecisive, doubtful, and torn as to which path to take. At a time in life when they feel the most imperfect, they don't want to hear perfection. Set the bar of expectation and achievement too high and they won't think they can meet it. They'll fill up with anger as they beat themselves up when they fall short. It's not uncommon for them to withdraw into unhealthy habits or friendships or give up and shut down or push you away.

Do you like being around people who are perfect? Or think they are? I don't. A condescending and arrogant person pushes me away. If they're fake and disingenuous they might be communicating their perfection. I prefer the presence of imperfect people who allow—no, who welcome and embrace—other imperfect people. And your grandkids do too.

MY PARENTS AND GRANDPARENTS ARE TOO AUTHORITARIAN

Parents and grandparents have God-given authority to parent kids. God placed kids in your life for a reason and a purpose. He placed you in their life for the same. How we communicate and use our position makes all the difference in the world to our grandkids.

Here's an example. I believe a policeman has achieved a position of authority in society. However, the way this officer of the law approaches his role makes all the difference in the way people respond to his authority. If he is relational, most people will respond accordingly. However, if this policeman comes across as a strong authoritarian, he will probably push more people away than gather them around him.

They may have to bend to his authority, but they don't have to like it—or him.

You are in the same position. Your exercise of authority determines your likeability to your grandkids. Your authoritarian approach isn't wrong—it's just ineffective because of the changing climate of the adolescent culture. Teens don't respect people in authority like they used to. When you reflect on what teens hear about pastors, police officers, politicians, coaches, teachers, and others in authority, it's not hard to understand that perception is *truth* to the one who perceives it.

That means whether I like it or not, whether I think it's right or wrong, the authoritarian approach to grandparenting doesn't work. That doesn't mean you give up your standards or compromise your values or faith. It just means a different angle can be much more effective with teens than a heavy-handed approach.

MY PARENTS AND GRANDPARENTS COME ACROSS AS JUDGMENTAL

Here's one for the guilt pile. Remember, it's how we are perceived by our grandkids that determines whether they think we are judgmental, which in today's politically correct culture is a pretty sensitive topic.

When you talk about race, homosexuality, couples living together, divorce, teachers, and police officers, how do you come across to your grandchildren? To the world? Is there a hint of judgment in your words or tone?

Not many years ago, we were able to say whatever we wanted. We used plenty of words that weren't politically correct and other expressions that today would be considered rude that we thought were kind of funny. When I'm with trusted friends, I can say what I want and express thoughts I would never say in front of my grandkids. That's because the world they are growing up in doesn't tolerate a hint of judgmental attitude toward anyone. It's not at all funny to them.

Is it right or is it wrong? It doesn't matter. If my grandchild feels I'm judgmental and that is getting between our relationship, no matter how much *freedom of speech* I have or how wrong they may be in curtailing my rights, I stop. I cherish this special relationship, and I don't want to do anything to damage it.

My grandkids are not just grandkids; I want them to be my brothers and sisters in Christ. I don't want to do anything to make them stumble.

In order to counter the ineffective ways of engagement with teens, I preface my comments. I use statements such as these at the beginning of many of our conversations, just so they know my intent.

- "I don't want you to be perfect but how do you want me to . . ."
- "I don't want to be pushy but you're putting me in a difficult position by . . ."
- "I don't mean to be judgmental so help me understand what is going on here."
- "I know we're all imperfect and I don't mean to come across as a know-it-all."
- "I want to hear you but I want you to hear the heart of what I say also."
- "I know we think differently about this so help me understand your view."

By prefacing what I want to say, I steer them away from thinking I demand perfection, act too authoritarian, or judge too much.

How do your grandkids perceive you? What would they say about the way you come across? Would they say you demand perfection? Would they say you rule the roost? Would they say you rule the family kingdom with an iron fist? Would they think you are somewhat judgmental?

Ask them. Text them and ask. Call them and ask. Don't be too chicken. I double-dog dare you.

Perhaps say it this way:

"Sweetheart, do you think I want you to be perfect?"
"Hey, do you feel like I come across pretty harsh and immovable sometimes?"

"I need to know something. Do you think I'm a judgmental person?"
"If you could change one thing about me, what would that be?"
*"What is one thing about our relationship you would like to be
    different?"*

Whatever their response, let it sit for a while. Then let them know
you'd like to get together and talk about how you are preventing your
relationship from growing. Let them know how much they mean to
you. Make a pact always to clear up, address, and discuss anything that
might come between this special relationship God has placed in your
lives. You'll be so glad you did.

Chapter 5

THE CHANCE TO BE A SUPERHERO (WHEN THEIR LIVES SUCK)

My message and my preaching were not with wise and persuasive

words, but with a demonstration of the Spirit's power, so that your

faith might not rest on human wisdom, but on God's power.

1 Corinthians 2:4–5 (NIV)

When Maile was sixteen, she texted me one time, "Poppa, can we get together for dinner? Just us?" I quickly responded that as soon as I got back in town from a speaking event, I would pick her up and we'd go wherever she wanted to eat. "Yes, sweetheart, in a heartbeat," I replied. When we sat down at a local restaurant, I could tell that she needed something more than just a discussion.

She just wanted to talk. Not really about anything remarkable or astounding. That wasn't her point. She was really asking, *Am I valuable and important enough that you'd like to get together?* I heard it loud and clear and quickly responded, "Yes."

One of these days, she'll ask if we can get together again, and it will be something remarkable, maybe earth-shattering. Those critical conversations will never occur unless I'm willing to talk now to build trust and affection first.

THOSE WHO'VE MEANT A LOT

I've said for years that it's not the presence of negative comments but the absence of positive comments that set one's life on its course. The positive for many kids is a grandparent who is just a listening ear. And when you think you're finished listening, you listen a bit more. Somewhere in the midst of wearing your ears out, a grandchild begins to believe you're a superhero. All because you showed up and helped just in the nick of time.

They'll remember your stories and bits of wisdom, just as you and I did growing up from the adults who spoke to us. From my early childhood up through my thirties, I was like a sponge soaking up anything I could and hanging on to every word coming from the mouths of these trusted men. These men helped me figure out who I was, what I was supposed to do, and what my purpose was in life. It might not have taken me so long if the voices I heard in my elementary and teen years had encouraged more than discouraged. My sponge soaked up quite a bit of negative criticism from people who were more skilled at finding fault than wisdom.

And they contradicted one another. Even after I became an adult, many other adults I knew spent time telling me what I couldn't do rather than what great things might be in store for my wife, Jan, and me. People said I shouldn't have dated Jan as long as I did. Some said we shouldn't have gotten married so early. We've now been married forty-five years. Some folks close to me said I shouldn't work for a church. I worked on a church staff for seven years. I met many parents who thought I was constantly wrong. In fact, I couldn't do anything right in their eyes. Many said moving to Branson, Missouri, to work for Young Life was a mistake. We spent seven years at this as well.

The biggest punch in the gut was when a trusted friend sat with me and told me he didn't think I was capable of starting Heartlight. He thought it would fail if I tried it.

I remember his exact words. "Mark, you don't have the ability. You don't have the resources. And you don't have the personality to pull this off." While I appreciated his honesty, I began to realize that he really wasn't that "trusted friend" I thought, and he really didn't know me like I thought he did. I began to think that his message was harsh, his timing was off, and I questioned his intent

He thought moving our little family to Texas was going to be a big mistake, and he stated I just wasn't capable of fulfilling the plans I thought God had for us.

In a way, he was right. I wasn't capable, but God was. He knew my calling, my passion, and my purpose. He created me for it.

The people described were naysayers, people who always saw the glass half-empty and who took one-way trips to Negative Town, always emphasizing the worst of any situation.

I knew older folks as I grew up who chose to sit with me and listen. All times of the day, any day of the week, they could be counted on to listen to my hopes and dreams, offering input only when I wanted it or asked for it. From them I learned some important lessons that came from their ability to use experience and knowledge to make good decisions and judgments. I'm sure they never realized the impact they were having on me. As I reflect on their effect on me, I guess their influence was what a grandparent could have offered me. These people cared more for me than my grandparents ever did, and they showed it by their encouraging message of what "I could be" rather than the discouraging verbiage of what "I wasn't."

I've spent a lot of time looking back on my life, thinking about those people who helped me become who I am. As I try to imagine what I would be without their words of wisdom, well, I just can't. Most of those guys are dead now. Some have lost their spouses. Others have lost their minds. I still keep in touch with a few. But all of their legacies live on in me.

When I worked as a youth pastor at the church in Tulsa, a fellow named Dave Tillack told me, "Mark, don't stoop to be a king when you're called to be a servant." Think about that one. For me, that was a totally different perspective from being told to put others ahead of myself—the same principle, but a new way of hearing and perceiving it.

The pastor of that church, Dr. L.D. Thomas, and I were out for lunch at the Tulsa Oil Club one time, and I remember him pointing to everyone in the room, saying, "Mark, every person in this room feels like they're carrying the weight of the world on their shoulders."

Another pastor there, Doug Burr, told me a number of times, "Mark, God's going to use you" whenever I found myself in difficult situations of having to perform a funeral of one of the teens in our youth group, or having to face a group of critical parents where I questioned my abilities.

I remember the radio preacher Chuck Swindoll saying, "Everything that has come to you has first passed through the hands of God."[2]

John Roberts, a swim coach I had for a number of years, said, "Mark, if you think you can, you will. If you think you can't, you won't. For many, a race was lost before the gun even sounded."

Smith Brookhart, a dear friend in Branson, Missouri, would remind me, "Markus, you're doing a good thing."

Spike White of Kanakuk Kamp, who took me under his wing, would say, "Mark, have you thanked the guy who fired you and brought you to Texas?"

Pete Herschend, another dear Branson friend, would say as we started Heartlight, "Mark, remember that your revenues will always be half of what you expect, and your expenses will be twice the amount you planned for."

Wishard Lemons told me when talking about ministry, "Mark, people in ministry don't laugh enough."

Joe Mooberry once said, "Mark, most Christian ministries cater to women; it's our job to serve up a good meal to men."

Cliff Taulbert shared with me over coffee, "Mark, you've got to be genuine, and you've got to be real, or people won't stand to be around you."

All of these folks probably don't even know the impact each simple-but-wise sentence had on me. I'm not sure I knew how important they were at the time. In hindsight, I see how each molded me and how God used them to influence me. It was these guys who left a legacy of hope for me. To each, I am most grateful.

THE LEGACY OF HOPE

I noticed how my grown-up superheroes didn't use scripture in every comment they made. However, each undoubtedly stood on biblical principles for their own lives. Sometimes wisdom is shared from the ways you internalize God's Word in your life. You naturally express it through golden statements based on your experience and knowledge.

In all their time with me, each of those people had similarities in their influence that presented a wonderful example to me. Now I can use my influence, in the same way, to share wisdom with my grandchildren. You can too. There are a few common practices to note:

- These one-liners didn't come out of just one meeting. They are nuggets I remember from a span of time we spent together. Conversations didn't set out to solve a specific problem at a specific time. They were just ongoing conversations over a long period of time.
- These friends were intentional about training me. These meetings weren't just to shoot the breeze or pass time. They recognized they had a sponge sitting there soaking up anything it could. They were purposeful (not agenda-driven), with a desire to pass on something that would make my life different.

- Time spent together was positive. At least, it seemed like it was. I'm sure they said things that needed to be said, but I always left our times together with a sense of encouragement, not discouragement.
- Each gave room for me to ask questions, millions of them. They weren't afraid to tell me answers I didn't want to hear, but they told them in an affirming way. I trusted them when they were right; I trusted them when they were wrong.
- These steadfast *rocks* had insight, meaning they processed their own experiences and drew out insight and wisdom to be passed on to others.
- They told stories. Their own stories of successes and failures, challenges and hurdles, and what they had learned or picked up in the process.
- No matter how I saw something, each always helped me see things from another perspective.
- Deep down, I knew each of these folks loved me and enjoyed the time we were able to spend together. I felt their commitment when they introduced me to friends, other colleagues, and folks we would bump into during our times together.
- They didn't spend time correcting me by telling me how I needed to do something different, now or next time. If they did, I think I would have checked out and put them in the same category as other naysayers in my life.
- They acted as a remedy, helping me figure out God's best for my life.

I'm sure you can list a very similar group of people who influenced your life. These guys were my superheroes. And God placed them in my life for a purpose. Now it's your turn to be that influencer, storyteller, perspective-giver, sharer of successes, communicator of failures, insight injector, and positive trainer. God placed your grandchild in your life for a reason.

And that reason might just be that you're to be their superhero!

Chapter 6

YOU DON'T GIVE UP WHEN THEY HURT YOUR HEART

And we know that God causes all things to work together

for good to those who love God, to those who

are called according to His purpose.

ROMANS 8:28 (NASB)

My son's phone call was expected. His message was not. "Dad, I'm getting divorced," he said.

I'm sure the neighbors could hear my response. "What do you mean, you're getting divorced? You just got married! What are you thinking?"

"I've met someone else," my son said.

I remember the intensity of my calm but strong words: "Well, Adam, when you can call your wife's father and apologize for screwing up her life, then I'll talk to you."

Doesn't that sound great? Wasn't it manly? I thought I was doing the right thing, standing up for what was right. I was defending what God desires and what we stood for as a family. Mind you, this was the same son who inspired the tagline of truth I've communicated to hundreds of thousands of parents—*There's nothing you can do to make me love you more, and nothing you can do to make me love you less.*

When my son needed me the most, I wasn't anywhere to be found. While he was lost, I let him wander. When he needed a dad who would walk with him through a difficult time, I wrote him off. During this difficult time, my presence in my son's life was lacking. Then I woke up one morning and realized what I thought I was doing in the name of righteousness wasn't working. The more I thought about it, the more I came to see how I put my expectations above my own son. I justified my behavior with the idealistic thoughts that I was doing what God wanted me to do. Boy, was I wrong.

Adam hurt me. When I turned my back on him, it was because of my own feelings. I was thinking more about myself and how I was going to lose a daughter-in-law whom I loved than I was about my son's turmoil. I did not consider the internal conflict and struggle he was going through. Yep, I put myself first.

I've spent hours of reflection since then looking in the rearview mirror. I believe God would have me spend more time trying to touch the hearts of those who are hurting me than protect my own heart or convince myself I am protecting God's very own heart by turning my back on any one of His precious kids.

A parent of one of the kids let me know he was disappointed in me. Said I wasn't standing up to the media and publicity he felt were exploiting his daughter. She was engaged in a same-sex relationship, and the media loved revealing this scandal. The media defamed him and his wife, and damaged Heartlight's reputation. The media were relentless and started making accusations that our program was into *conversion therapy.*

Eventually, I decided it would be best for this man's daughter to leave our program. It wasn't working for any of us. With the relentless pounding of the media, there was no solution for either of us. That publicity could bring problems to other families and teens entrusted to us at that time.

This father and mother are dear people who love their daughter immensely. The father caught me somewhat off guard with what he said when he came to pick her up at my request. "This approach is not what I would have expected. It gives the impression of fear, not confidence in the Lord's provision." He felt we should fight not only for his daughter but also against the homosexual agenda. I disagreed. That is not Heartlight's mission. I just didn't think that was our fight to take on a cause against a turning culture when it didn't include us.

His comment got me thinking quite a bit about what stand we are supposed to take when we encounter people and situations that don't follow what we believe. Scripture says the following:

> *But you, man of God, flee from all this, and pursue righteousness, godliness, faith, love, endurance and gentleness.* Fight the good fight *of the faith. Take hold of the eternal life to which you were called when you made your good confession in the presence of many witnesses.* (1 TIMOTHY 6:11–12, *emphasis added*)

I believe the fight mentioned here means fights and quarrels that get us up caught up in arguing over things that create nothing eternal. Matter of fact, I further believe this scripture is pretty targeted at encouraging people to fight the good fight that pursues righteousness, godliness, faith, love, endurance, and gentleness. All these things are eternal.

I don't think this scripture means I am to fight everything that doesn't line up with God's Word. That lines up with a fight or brawl, with a winner and a loser.

I also don't think this scripture tells me I must fight other people's battles. Some people really believe it is their job to create or finish any and all fights. I don't. Some admirable and honorable battles just aren't my business. Love might get lost in the fight and I'd lose time for others. When we fight and win relationships, we both win. There's nothing wrong with fighting for a cause. It's just that some of those causes aren't mine to fight.

So where does this come into grandparenting?

YOU AND YOUR PEERS ARE GETTING OLDER

You are getting older. You have things you believe in and a number of things you don't believe in.

As this new and changing culture emerges, don't confuse love and listening as acceptance. No one is saying you have to embrace what you believe is sin. It's just that sometimes (I would argue most times) we need to let the Holy Spirit be in charge of making those we love *accountable* for their sins. That's the Spirit's job anyway, isn't it? Who made it ours?

It's easy to get caught up in some of the quarrels and controversies that are more about fighting than they are about resolution. Maybe the way you believe is different from the way your grandchild believes. You can spend the time fighting, and both lose relationship, goodwill, and love as I just said. Or you can love in spite of the differences and without losing your special relationship.

Here's what the Bible states right before that verse about fighting the good fight:

They have an unhealthy interest in controversies and quarrels about words that result in envy, strife, malicious talk, evil suspicions and constant friction between people. (1 TIMOTHY 6:4–5)

My message is simple. Don't fight for something that produces nothing.

Some situations may be hard to swallow but show how much you love your grandchildren in spite of your differences. Think about these possibilities before you face any of them so you don't react negatively when you find out what's going on. Think about these now so you can keep your head on straight if any of them occurs within your precious family.

You have to figure out how you would respond when you first hear that your grandson or granddaughter is gay or bisexual.

You might have to live with fact that your granddaughter doesn't want the same kind of relationship that you have with God. Or maybe not want any relationship at all.

You may have to accept the fact that your grandson is living with his girlfriend. What do you say?

You will probably have a grandchild who thinks it is okay to smoke pot. Will you let the difference in how you feel about something that has no eternal value determine (or destroy) the relationship you have with your grandchild?

If you differ on politics, the changing climate, or same-sex marriage, do you think you can share wisdom about these hot topics when there is disagreement on the particulars?

Can you still participate and attend a grandchild's wedding if the couple is already expecting a baby?

Can you still love a grandson or granddaughter who sees nothing wrong with smoking, gambling, drinking, or other violations of your standards?

Will your granddaughter still feel the specialness of the relationship with you if she is just a little immodest and parties more than you ever would have wanted?

These scenarios are easy to read on the page, much harder when they hit home. When any of these scenarios happen within *your* family, what will your reaction be? Hopefully, these situations do not just spring on you, but are preceded by a few conversations and time for you to give wise (and sensitive) input when it counts the most. You have an opportunity to help form opinions and beliefs, rather than just being a recipient of your grandchild's announcements or a bystander watching behavior you think is inappropriate.

A LIGHT IN THEIR DARKNESS

Your relationship is key. The God of relationships calls you to be a light in the darkness. Your words of encouragement can be a rudder that steers even the mightiest of ships to a different destination. And your shared perspective might just spark a larger fire of passion for your grandchild's purpose in life.

You may think, *Okay, how do we do that, Mark? How do we approach a subject or situation that is contrary to what we believe without alienating our grandchild?*

Yes, they will listen to you, but only if you have already established a solid relationship where you are a trusted source of wisdom. If you haven't built the relationship, I doubt your opinion can make much difference and it will probably just create more distance. Chances are, your grandchild already knows what you believe regarding the situations I listed a few paragraphs previously, and their fear is that they will disappoint you and you will condemn them.

Your approach to your grandchildren at critical times shows what your relationship can withstand. More than you think.

If your grandchildren live close to you, it will be easier to communicate on a regular basis. Grandkids who are geographically distant present more of a challenge. If you only get to spend time together a couple of visits a year, it becomes a little trickier. In that situation, you may want to invite them to go on special trips, vacations, or weekend expeditions. FaceTime or Skype as often as you can. Make sure you find the time to talk. And keep pursuing them with reminders that you desire to be a part of their life.

As your grandkids reach their teen years and beyond and you need to talk about something tough, I'd approach the discussion by saying, "You and I know I'm old, and I don't see things in the same way perhaps much of the world accepts. We're different, you and I, but we have had and always will have a special relationship. Right now, I want to speak to the *elephant in the room*. Tell me what's going on in your life. I would love to know what you're thinking."

That should get you in the door to keep the conversation going. Remember to ask questions. Whatever the answer (however misguided in your eyes), ask more questions. Hopefully, after you spend a period of time listening, your grandchild will ask you something along the lines of, "What do you think?"

- "What do you think about me living with my girlfriend?"
- "What do you think about me taking a year off after high school and traveling around the country?"
- "What do you think about me not coming home for Christmas, but going skiing instead?"
- "What do you think about what's happening in the country today?"
- "What do you think about politics today?"

Be careful here. I find sometimes it just isn't a good idea to share your opinions. Many times I look at kids when they ask a question and say, "It really doesn't matter what I think. I'm happy for you, and you know I'll never let any of your decisions get in the way of us."

There's a scripture that states,

Fools have no interest in understanding; they only want to air their own opinions. (PROVERBS 18:2, *NLT*)

That reminds me to wait when I am asked for my opinion. I need to consider first, *Am I being a fool? Do I want to understand my grand-children? Did I really hear their hearts, or was I formulating my own counter arguments the whole time they shared?* Sometimes my opinion is just not needed. Other times it may instill a sense of disappointment in my grandchild.

Let me ask you this. Once you hit your teen years, didn't you know your own sin better than anyone? Did you hide things from parents or even trusted friends? If anyone *caught* you or *condemned* you for your choices, did it help? Most of the time, teens know exactly what they are doing wrong in their lives. In fact, often they feel worse about themselves than they really are. They feel worse about their mistakes and failures than you could ever make them feel. If they are making poor choices in some areas and have been *brought up better*, then they most likely already think the ones they love see them as utter failures, not just human beings who mess up sometimes. They don't need to hear it. They need to be loved and encouraged through it.

That verse in Proverbs directs me at times to simply respond with, "I understand." They may say, "So you're okay with me doing [whatever it is they are doing]?" My response is, "I didn't say I agree with you. I said I understand, and we can still love each other and not agree with everything you're doing."

If I sense my opinion or perspective will be ignored at that time, then I don't share it. I can still wholeheartedly love and embrace a grandchild who doesn't want or take my advice.

THAT HURTS

One big key to parenting and grandparenting is: *Don't take it personally*. After all you have tried to teach and instill in them, their sin and poor choices can certainly feel personal. When your grandchildren hurt themselves or damage their lives or the lives of others, of course, it hurts you. It hurts badly sometimes. But you can't make your hurt the focus, or you will lash out in ways that won't be welcome. Put your hurt feelings aside for now. You're the grown-up.

I encourage you first to let parents handle some of the confrontations and deal with the conflict that arises when a grandchild makes seriously bad choices. It's the parents' fight. Your role is to encourage the parents (your kids) when they need it, let them know you want to come alongside them and help (not interfere), and be that safe place your grandchild can come and feel like they can discuss anything. Anything.

Because you've no doubt already experienced more than a few times when your own kids hurt your heart, you can handle situations with your grandkids a little differently. Where you missed it with your daughter, you can be right on with your granddaughter. Where you screwed up with your son, you can do better with your grandson. In a way, grandchildren give you a chance for a do-over.

Oh, and my son Adam? He married again, as did his ex-wife. He married a girl he loves dearly, and my ex-daughter-in-law married soon after. They are both happy. They both posted on Facebook the same day announcing the birth of their kids. Out of the thousands of Facebook friends I have, their posts were listed right underneath each other. What are the chances of that?

It was like God was saying regardless of whether I like the circumstances and the pain, He creates passion and purpose out of them. I stand witness to how He does it for thousands of teens who spend time at Heartlight. He will do it for your grandchildren and you.

—PART II—

THEY WILL LISTEN WHEN YOU TALK

Chapter 7

GIVING YOUR GRANDKIDS AN EAR

Tell your children about it in the years to come,

and let your children tell their children.

Pass the story down from generation to generation.

JOEL 1:3 (NLT)

Your grandkids are bombarded by so many messages and attitudes about life today. There are so many voices "speaking" to them, they sometimes have a hard time discerning what is truth and what is not. That's why they need you. A voice of truth. A relationship that will listen.

This is not a lost cause. One might think with the ever-increasing dependency on new technology and gadgets to communicate that you as a grandparent are becoming more and more obsolete. But that's not true. In reality, as technology expands, you are needed all the more to maintain those relationships that have been so special in the lives of your grandchildren. So don't give up. You can fight this, and you can win if you understand the world they live in and hone your skills to listening to the real needs of your grandkids.

Teens communicate differently today than we did when we were teens. The internet ushered in a new way not only of communicating, but also finding information, answers to questions, instructions to live by, entertainment that never quits, and new ways of social networking. Teens may think they are making tons of friends on the World Wide Web. They may feel as if they are communicating with the whole world. However, the reality is that talking, making friends, commenting, and meeting on the internet isn't the same as talking face-to-face, sharing meals, getting together, and hanging out. These newly found internet *relationships* many times lack real involvement and investment in one another's lives.

A CULTURE OF NEGATIVITY

There's a benefit to filling out surveys, writing reviews, stating opinions, and reflecting on experiences. There's something to be said for critiquing services, rating the performance of a business, or sharing a perspective or opinion on just about anything. People want to be heard, and the internet now provides a way to speak, regardless of whether or not anyone is listening. Quite honestly, I think this right to expression and accusatory demeanor will remain part of our culture for years to come. The negative side of this effort to rate every business, every politician, and every service is we have become a world where too many consider themselves *judge and jury.*

Given time, anyone can find fault with anything. There will be a bad meal served at a restaurant that has served thousands of great meals. There will always be mistakes, shortcomings, disappointments, and unmet expectations as long as man is alive. If you look hard enough and deep enough into anybody's background, you can find faults, discover disappointments, learn about their mistakes, and obtain information that can be misused to trash them. The negativity of the culture has exploded. People are critical, complaining, "yelping," rating everyone's performance, and sharing opinions publicly.

People do have the right to complain. But it doesn't mean they should. To me, constant complaining counters the first verses of Matthew 7, which state,

Judge not, that you be not judged. For with what judgment you judge, you will be judged; and with the measure you use, it will be measured back to you. And why do you look at the speck in your brother's eye, but do not consider the plank in your own eye? (MATTHEW 7:1–3, *NKJV*)

Today we live in a culture that considers negativity just *being real.* The problem with negativity being the norm lies in the fact that it creates an absence of positive messages to counterbalance the constant stream of bad stuff. In other words, so much time is spent focusing on and explaining the negative that little time is spent clarifying and illuminating anything positive. Teens don't hear positives anymore. They hear where they failed, didn't measure up, and what they need to do better next time.

AN ATMOSPHERE OF KNOW-IT-ALLS

Second, this culture of negativity is filled with know-it-alls and self-proclaimed authorities; they really believe they've cornered and mastered certain roles because they've tried or experienced something once or twice. Sharing personal experiences becomes a platform interpreted as wise and authoritative merely because it is videoed, blogged about, or printed.

I didn't write this book based on what I learned from being a grandparent. What gives me the platform to speak on grandparenting is my work with thousands of families. I have seen firsthand the significant impact and ways grandparents are indeed creating a legacy of influence for their grandchildren.

I've seen plenty of videos and blogs of new fathers sharing what they are learning about fatherhood. They have infants, and they are already online telling everyone else how they should parent. Suddenly these new dads are the experts. I've seen and listened to many who adopted one child. Now they evidently know how to counsel everyone else on how to raise an adopted child. It's like everyone has suddenly become experts. A blog is practically viewed as a doctoral degree, allowing just about anyone to think he is a specialist because of one experience.

That's about as sensible as calling me a veterinarian because I helped a vet sew up one of our horses who had a deep cut. Or calling me an obstetrician because I delivered my own son. Maybe I'm a preacher because I spoke in a pulpit. I'm not a dentist just because I brushed my teeth this morning.

Sharing one's perspective does not make one a professional. Her own personal story alone does not give the writer or blogger the credentials to lead others. As grandparents, we know this because we've been around the block a few times and understand that, just because you see something or read something doesn't mean it's automatically the truth. It does not mean it is totally accurate either. It's just one person's perspective based on what they saw or felt.

Teens are falling hook, line, and sinker for many people's foolishness because they know no better. They interpret information as wisdom. They can hardly tell the difference between the two.

Two things happen when everyone is a know-it-all or a so-called expert. One, it creates a world of false wisdom. Two, it inflates many people to believe they know more than they really do.

A WORLD OF FANTASY

Third, a many teens and even young adults are happy to stay holed up in their bedrooms posting their observations, hopes, and a whole lot of selfies on social media rather than go out and meet with the real world. They remain where they are rather than moving forward to a better situation in life. Change takes self-discipline and drive, and they don't have any to help them improve, grow, and mature. They use social media posts and affirmations as validation they are doing great, when in reality they may not be.

Here's an example. I recently saw a post on Facebook where a young man on our staff stated he finally felt content with his life. He had found new confidence to face everything before him. He stated he used to be goofy with his words, crazy in his actions, and immature in the way he related to people. He added that he used to view his appearance negatively, but now is satisfied and pleased with where he is.

I was excited for this young man as he had developed a new view of himself. But then I read the comments from all his *friends*, and they alarmed me. All 110 of them affirmed everything this young man was feeling. And while that sounds great on the surface, the truth is, he still struggles with many of the same issues he now thinks he *used* to have. In their desire to stay on trend, the friends' comments completely skipped over the truth. I don't think social media is the right forum to speak the truth in love, and if this young man takes these comments to the bank, he's not going to progress in real-life settings.

Truthfully, this guy is an amazing young man. But he can be obnoxious and act out for attention. And, if he doesn't make some changes physically, he'll likely face serious health problems in the future. My concern is that none of the "encouraging comments" left in his social media feed really addressed some much needed issues that need to be talked about if any of these friends are serious about helping him. Again, I'm glad that no one called him out on social media, but if he counts on these messages as his only belief system, then he is headed for failure in his future days.

There needs to be someone in this young man's life who speaks the kind of truth that can help him create better relationships with others, find significance, and go places to use his gifts and talents. Contentment quickly changes to complacency when one is not challenged to do better. Then many times, motivation to move on to a better place gets lost. My fear is that he'll live a lost life, not becoming all he was meant to be for the lack of loving, kind, and truthful interaction in his life.

This new culture is difficult for teens to navigate. On the one hand, the cultural tone (political, doom-and-gloom attitudes about the climate, gender wars, left vs. right, and more) is so negative it has teens worried, walking on pins and needles about their futures. False information from so-called experts leads them to second-guess what they hear and read. People commit horrific acts such as rape and murder and broadcast them live on social media. On the other hand, teens' social media circles go overboard in their praise of what is sometimes patently ridiculous.

It's like that old children's fable of the emperor and his new clothes. At the end of the story, the emperor marches through the streets naked, foolishly convinced he is wearing fine garments. Even more foolishly, his subjects all pretend he is fully clothed too. They praise the beautiful new outfit the emperor wears, and he is stark naked as a jaybird.

Even though teens want to believe it, fake affirmation causes them not to trust what they hear, wondering whether they are really being told the truth.

This cultural struggle provides a perfect setting for grandparents to enter. In a world of negatives, know-it-alls, and half-truths, your grandchild is looking for a positive, trustworthy speaker of the truth in love. Your voice of tried-and-true experience can rise above the white noise that drowns out sensible and wise advice. That's your call. Will you accept it?

You can be a voice in the darkness of this world that gently offers what your grandkids are searching for desperately. Speak truth, whether they seem like they are listening or not. When they hear something completely different from those around them, but they're not quite sure who to believe, your history with them of love and support can convince them you're the one who's telling it straight.

GIVING YOUR GRANDKIDS WHAT THEY WANT (EVEN WHEN THEY DON'T KNOW THEY WANT IT)

Grandkids don't come to grandparents to get more information. They usually come to ask questions. They are seeking insight and direction. This offers the perfect opportunity for you to share your mistakes, failures, and struggles. After all, they are the source of much of your wisdom.

Quite honestly, information is a dime a dozen. It can be found anywhere and shared by anyone. Google, Siri, or Alexa can provide facts and details. That kind of stuff is not what your grandchildren are looking or hoping for. Again, they are looking for wisdom, the ability to use experience and knowledge to make good decisions and judgments. Information is communicated in the teaching model; wisdom is shared in the training model.

One of my greatest concerns for teens today is how many are viewing scripture as information, not wisdom. Because they're in an information world, they categorize scripture as just another historical reference, a good story, more material to process, a mere set of data that is part of their family tradition.

What they want to know is how scripture relates to them. How can the Bible help them get to a great place in life? The wisdom from the scriptures needs to be presented in a way that seems applicable to their real lives. Grandparents can share that.

For example, scripture clearly states sex within marriage is the only form of sexual relations of which God approves (see Hebrews 13:4, 1 Thessalonians 4:3, Jude 7, Colossians 3:5, Galatians 5:19, 1 Corinthians 5:1, 2 Corinthians 12:21). For many teens, this is just information from a dusty document. How does it work today? Why would it make sense to swim against a very sexualized culture when sex is fun? Everybody's doing it. Everybody's flaunting it. "Why should we deny ourselves?"

Here's where they need wisdom—the wisdom you have and can give. This wisdom is more than repeating the scriptures they already know. This wisdom explains why this principle should be followed. It gives practical examples of the benefits and drawbacks of following the culture or following the Bible. A grandparent might communicate the wisdom packed in these verses in the following way:

> "In all my years, I've heard and lived by the same principles my parents taught me. This is what I found. Sex before marriage has an unbelievable way of causing confusion in relationships. So if this is the girl you're going to one day marry, make sure you do whatever is necessary not to confuse the relationship. Work hard to not 'muddy the waters' with the one you will spend the rest of your life with."

This sample conversation includes not only the truth and information they've been given but lets them hear the importance of this principle. It emphasizes how it is relevant to them. In a world of information bombardment, can you dig deep and give them wisdom? Help them leave your table of conversation satisfied, not hungry, so they won't accept phony substitutes or shallow facts to satisfy their longings.

This wisdom is usually shared through stories of failures, successes, and lessons learned. These transform information into true-to-life experiences that can affect their choices and selections in life. Share your wisdom with intentionality. Don't just blow smoke in their ears. You don't tell the stories of your life for the satisfaction of telling them. (Remember the old folks who detailed their health ailments and scared their grandchildren and me away?) You tell them to offer a balance in their unbalanced world. You tell them to speak the truth in love, with affirmations of good and encouragement to mature in areas of much-needed growth.

THE ART OF STORYTELLING

Most times, wisdom and hope are shared through stories that include a concept or nugget of truth that sticks in your grandchildren's minds because the stories give them something they enjoy and want to hear.

Do you tell good stories? Can you think of the funniest moments in your life? How about the most bittersweet? What did you learn from the best and worst times of your life? What memories bring a smile to your face? What tales could grab the attention of your grandchild as you sit around the dinner table or in front of a fireplace talking? Your life stories help your grandchild get to know you better, but they can also help them examine their own lives in light of the choices you made.

Surely you have plenty of stories you can weave into *parables*. A parable is a story with a lesson of right and wrong. Make sure each of your stories has a punch line of truth, a lesson to be learned that they will remember. Don't overdo it.

Making kids laugh is wonderful. It's a true gift when you can attach a life truth that you gathered and now want to pass along. Earlier, I mentioned a comment made to me that changed my life. A dear fellow named Dave Tillack told a story. Then he said the infamous line (for me it was, anyway) that stuck with me.

"When you're called to be a servant, don't stoop to be a king," Dave said.

He knew my heart to serve, and he was affirming my desire to be a servant, which is a far better position than one of being a king. I don't remember the story or the context in which he was speaking, but I will forever remember that one line.

Some of the memorable stories I tell teens are the ones where I share my own humanity. I admit my mistakes and struggles. I reveal my vulnerability. I've learned to pull the humor out of all those stories, and I aim to keep it to one point per story. Ten lessons in one tale either would make the story uninteresting (like a lecture) or too hard to take in and apply.

Practice your stories, even out loud in front of the mirror. Think about the funniest comedians. They take real-life situations and bring out the extraordinary. They admit when they acted foolishly or saw other people do something silly. They practice these routines again and again. Then they perform them over and over, honing and perfecting their craft. The best comics leave us wanting more by bringing their humorous anecdotes back around to something more serious. They leave us with a heartfelt lesson they learned. We love their routines because we can relate.

Think back over your life. Jot down some stories or say them into a voice recorder. Play them back. Are they funny? Or judgmental? Do they have a subtle message? Try out your stories on your spouse or kids and tell them you want to share them with the grandkids. What's their response? You can leave a legacy of life lessons shared in the most entertaining ways. That's what I try to do with my own grandkids. I want my grandkids to say, "Remember when Poppa told us about...?" Or, "Hey, Poppa, tell us the story about ...."

I find most truths transfer best through stories, ones that are unique in origin and simple in approach. A story is easy to remember. Share yours. Include a point but don't give it away too easily. Let them figure out how it applies to their own lives.

THE INTENTIONALITY OF SHARING WISDOM

I'm convinced sharing wisdom doesn't always come naturally and doesn't transfer just by *hanging out*. Grandparents must choose to be intentional in order to impart something special that brings wisdom to lives of their grandchildren.

I was on the phone recently with a man who said he was going to hang out with his granddaughter over the weekend. He planned to spend some time with her as this twelve-year-old struggled to handle her parents' divorce. Her school performance had slipped, her appetite had fled, her interest in her extracurricular activities had waned, and she had isolated herself. She wanted to quit the activities she loved.

Her granddad wanted to help her get through this tragic time in her life by hanging out, but this young lady needed some guidance and direction. That takes more than just hanging out. Her actions (or inactivity) and attitudes showed clearly she was asking for help and a little bit of hope. This well-meaning grandpa planned to offer a time of activities and entertainment but trying to cheer his granddaughter up or distract her from her problems wasn't going to fix the big issue in her life.

I encouraged the granddad to spend some time having fun, but also to plan a time to sit down and open the door to share some wisdom. Maybe it could take place at an ice cream stand, a coffee shop, or her favorite pizza place. But he needed to create an atmosphere of connection more than just fun and activity.

When you have moments to sit down and enjoy each other's company, but a larger issue like divorce still needs to be addressed, I would say something like the following.

"Sweetheart, I know it's tough when a family is going through a divorce. I know it's a little complicated and you have so many feelings inside your head and heart. I want you to know if you ever need to talk to someone who has big ears and can listen well, I'm here for you. We can have fun, as I always do with you. But I want you to know I'm not afraid to talk about the tough stuff that you're going through too. Understand what I'm saying?"

She may not say anything other than, *uh-huh*. But at the very least, in this situation, the granddaughter knows her grandparent is available to listen and offer hope. Over time, grandkids come back and share with grandparents who invite them to do so. If you don't offer anything more than a good time, grandkids might believe you only want to keep things light and can't deal with the harder things in life. Or they might feel you love them when all is going well but can't (and won't) handle them when anything is wrong. Walk the tightrope of conversational wisdom with your grandchildren. If you fall, get back up and try again.

EXPOSING THE TRUTH IN LOVE

Teens need to hear the truth in a way that does not feel judgmental or cloaked as a demand for perfection. It's a delicate dance. Grandparents need to learn not to gloss over what is going on in their grandkids' lives with total praise and good times together, but also to tread lightly at first when introducing heavy subjects. Give them the opportunity to come to you anytime, and don't push or prod too hard. When you strike the right balance, grandkids feel comfortable having deeper discussions.

Grandparents need to land right in the middle, not an authoritarian who points out every imperfection and not the loving people who see everything their grandchildren do as sunshine and roses.

One point about proximity: if you only see your grandchildren once a year, then those times need to be times of affirmation and encouragement. Listen more than talk, ask questions rather than giving answers, and don't focus on dumping on them or getting everything out in the air you heard they're doing wrong.

When you do speak to an issue, make sure you do so in a spirit of love. Don't talk about sore subjects when you are angry. Most likely they'll still be there once you cool off. Approach tough subjects with the intent to help. You are not in their lives to prove to yourself or anyone else that your way of handling their messes and mistakes is the only right way. You are there to support, encourage, compliment parents in correction, and communicate calm wisdom.

Here are some things you can cross off your list. Phrases such as these will only offend and push your grandchildren away:
- "You look like you're gaining weight."
- "Why can't you do things like your brother/sister?"
- "I told you so."

- "If you only used your head."
- "Well, your actions aren't telling me anything different!"
- "You always do this!" or, "You never do that!"
- "I don't think you can do it."
- "Did you wash your hair this morning?"
- "Why don't you have better friends?"

All of these are veiled judgments in the form of questions. They may hold truth, but they do not communicate love and acceptance. You can try to retract hurtful statements immediately, but they won't be forgotten. Kids internalize harsh statements immediately. Your apology may be accepted, but the sting remains. If you ever have to explain what you mean, then you should have done your homework and discovering what shame is to a kid.

Shame-based comments push teens further into inappropriate behavior they are exhibiting to cover the inadequacy they feel. A well-spoken word counters insecurity, inadequacy, and negativity. It gives values to the one who hears it. Positive words say, "You matter." When words damage and harm, the one who said them quickly gets put on the list of teens' favorite people to avoid.

Here's what one young man shared about his grandfather. Which category did he put his Grandpa in?

"Grandpa always listened to me first. Then he would share a story that made his perspective interesting. He had an unbelievable way of being positive when he was sharing something negative about me. He looked me straight in the eye, and I knew I was loved, listened to, and corrected in a way that made me always want to come back for more."

Wow! That is high praise from a teen. Believe me. Don't you want your grandchildren to describe you in those terms? If so, speak to their issues with a great sense of love. Be intentional about taking advantage of the time you have to share wisdom. Pull them out of their fantasy worlds of social media and into real life. Practice your stories and tell them with laughter and a great message.

You can be the one who counters the culture of negativity. You can be grandparents who bring balance to the off-kilter world your grandkids live in.

Chapter 8

WON'T SOMEBODY JUST LISTEN!

Do nothing out of selfish ambition or vain conceit. Rather, in

humility value others above yourselves, not looking to your

own interests but each of you to the interests of the others.

PHILIPPIANS 2:3–4 (NIV)

*I*f there was ever a time that adolescents are looking for someone to listen, it is now. Over the last few years, effective communication and discussion have depended on focusing on others more than yourself.

Let me use an example of a well-known group called Black Lives Matter, an organization formed in 2012. It works to validate Black lives. The slogan "Black Lives Matter" hit the news media a few years ago, and the immediate response was "All Lives Matter" from many across the country. This slogan became a springboard for other various slogans such as "Blue Lives Matter," "Gay Lives Matter," and "Firefighters' Lives Matter." The focus of public response was shifted to other groups who tried to invalidate the Black Lives Matter message by stating that others' lives matter just as much.

Now don't think this is a political statement. Please don't take my comments as a justification for anyone, and don't focus on the purpose and mission of any of these groups. I'm just pointing out the responses to this organization. I hardly know what any of the groups mentioned above believe or promote. It's just that I thought it odd that one group wanted to be heard and shared their concern, and many chose to respond with their own favorite slogan rather than listen. Many missed the original message the Black Lives Matter group was trying to communicate. In terms of true communication, the public's response was about as legitimate and effective as the following example.

My wife tearfully came to me years ago and in so many words said, "Mark, I was sexually abused for a number of years." If my response had been insensitive, "Well, Jan, there were a lot of people who were sexually abused," I'm sure it would have significantly affected our relationship and marriage. Her message would have been missed, her heart not heard because of my insensitivity and my need to respond rather than listen.

Or if one of the boys who live with us at Heartlight came up to me and shared that he had been sexually abused by a babysitter and all I did was tell him that a lot of guys (and girls) are assaulted by their babysitters, I doubt they would ever come and share anything with me again.

When people aren't heard, they start to scream the message louder. When that louder message isn't heard, then they become activists, actively behaving in a way to get other people's attention. Can you relate the same type of behavior to struggling teens? How about struggling grandchildren?

THE KEY TO ACTIVE LISTENING

The key to active listening is to understand what you hear. Our filters interpret and translate how we hear the message coming from our grandchild. Our filters might include how we were raised, our traditions, our hurts, our perceptions, our background, our own beliefs, and our values. Our own trust issues, our age, and our experiences can taint the messages we hear.

The challenge is to remove our filters and listen through our grandchildren's grid. We need to understand where they are coming from, not filter what they're saying through where we've been. If we hear it how they're saying it, then we'll be connecting.

Make it your goal to understand your grandchildren's world and filter their messages in the ways that look out for their interests, not your own. Effective grandparents are good listeners who possess the ability to look to the interests of their grandchildren in the grandchildren's world and not lean on their own understanding of their own world. That's called participatory listening.

Your interaction with your grandchild has got to be about them, not about you. A good listener has the ability to let people know they matter without saying a word. Good listeners have the amazing ability to speak to the heart because they understand where the hearts of their grandchildren are.

STOPPING CONVERSATIONS ON A DIME

Let's repeat some of the most common obstacles to conversations and offer some practical ways to improve your listening skills with your grandchildren.

Invite Them Over

How you respond to your grandchildren early in life will determine how they respond to you later in life. Isn't it ironic how annoyed we can get when our younger grandkids always want something, ask for everything, and never quit talking? Then they enter their teen years, and we wish they would tell us what they want, ask us questions, and maintain discussions with us?

Let your teen grandkids know you are still there for them. They can come on over anytime. When you're sitting around the dinner table, let them know you would love to hear what they have to say. When they speak, make eye contact to let them know you are listening.

Listen Now—Don't Wait

Timing is everything. If the opportunity to listen arises, make it a priority. When grandchildren want to talk, don't put them off or let it go until the weekend. If they have something on their hearts, then give them the opportunity to share it with you as soon as possible. Putting them off only sends the message that they just aren't important right now. If you find yourself always saying, "Let's talk later," you're missing some connecting opportunities.

Understand, Not Necessarily Agree

Chances are you are anywhere from forty-five to seventy years older than your grandchildren. That is a huge age difference Call it a generation gap, if you will. There are just differences—differences that will come up in your discussions.

When you start talking, let them know it is okay not to agree on everything. It's essential that the goal of your discussions is to bring you guys to understanding, not necessarily agreement.

When my grandkids want to have a discussion about a serious topic, whether it be abortion, marijuana, terrorism, war, or politics, I say this to them first, "I know that we won't agree on everything, but by helping me understand how you think, you may move me closer to appreciating your viewpoint."

This comment diffuses any potential argument. A comment such as this lets your grandchildren know you don't want to argue. You want to discuss. Discussion stoppers and *fighting words* include, but are certainly not limited to, the following:

- Where did that come from?
- Who told you that?
- Are you kidding me?
- That's stupid.
- Did you come up with that on your own?
- That's hard to believe!
- That's wrong.

Some comments that help your conversation move forward positively are more along the lines of these:

- That's interesting.
- Wow, that's different.
- I never thought of that.
- Hmm . . . .
- I see where you're coming from.
- I've never heard it said that way before.

Hey, when I'm having a discussion with a grandchild, or any kid for that matter, I want to do all I can to ensure the conversation is interesting and will be one we can continue in the future.

Don't Interrupt—It's a No-No

When you interrupt mid-sentence, interject a thought, or just blurt out what you're thinking and don't let your grandchildren complete their comments, you tell them you aren't listening. You're not valuing them.

Let them finish their sentences and comments. You worked hard to get this fire going. Don't put it out with interruptions that douse any chance you'll have for further conversations.

If you're both interrupters, one practical tool is to pass an object back and forth. Give your grandchildren a penny, a rock, a dollar, or whatever object you choose. Tell them you won't speak or respond to what they're saying until they pass you the chosen object. When you have the object, they can't speak.

And what's more, don't correct them during conversations. Ever been in conversations where there's so much correction going on you forget what the subject of the conversation was in the first place? Correction quickly becomes a distraction from the conversation your grandchild tries to have with you. Conversational correction looks a lot like this:

Grandchild: Grandpa, we spent two hours at the swimming pool.
Grandma: No, it was one-and-a-half hours.
Grandchild: Okay. And I swam six laps on my own.
Grandma: No, it was only four.
Grandchild: Okay. Then we left to get a hamburger.
Grandma: No, you had a hot dog.
Grandchild: Okay, we came home, and I took a nap for an hour.
Grandma: No, it was 30 minutes.

What happens in these situations is that eventually the child will have a conversation only in the presence of one grandparent, avoiding the corrector's presence. Most grandkids would rather not share anything than have a discussion full of correction. If you are one of those grandparents who is trying to get recognition or validation to show your grandchild that you are "of value" by constantly correcting,

I would suggest you try bringing value to the conversation, not getting your value from it.

Bring Value to the Conversation

For years, so many grandparents held jobs where people listened, valued their opinions, and couldn't wait to hear what they had to say. Then they retired, and no one wants to listen to what they have to say. They feel like they've lost their value. They no longer contribute. If you miss the validation you used to get from your job, you may try to recoup it in your conversations with those around you now (usually your spouse, kids, and grandkids). Are you bringing value to the conversation or just communicating to yourself for yourself?

You don't have to prove your value. You are exempt from having to do so because you are a grandparent. You don't have to prove anything to anyone. You are already valued because of who you are and how God values you. Your grandkids show you the value you hold by merely coming to you for wisdom, to ask questions, or to sit in your presence and hear your stories. You are more than important, more than valuable. You are invaluable. It is something that you already "are" . . . it's not something that you have to spend time "doing."

Repeat Back What They Just Said

Remember the age difference between you and your grandkids I wrote about earlier? If you're striving to understand what they are saying, but you're not sure you get it, repeat what you hear back to them. It's called "reflective listening."

> *"Okay, this is what I'm hearing you say. Am I getting it right?"*
> *"Is this what I'm hearing you communicate?"*

It keeps discussion on track. It prevents you from wandering on tangents. It repeats what they've said and helps them put their feelings into words.

Or try this other technique that I've found to be most helpful in "digging deeper" into the life of a teen. Ask a question that is general in nature. Take whatever they answer and put those words into another question. When they answer again, then take that answer and put into another question. It's like this:

Grandpa: How was your week this past few days?
Teen: It wasn't that good.
Grandpa: Why wasn't it good?
Teen: Things just kind of fell apart.
Grandpa: What things fell apart?
Teen: My girlfriend broke up with me.
Grandpa: Why did she break up with you?
Teen: Girls always break up with me.
Grandpa: Why do girls always break up with you?
Teen: I've always been controlling.
Grandpa: Why have you always been controlling?
Teen: Because I feel everything else is spinning out of control.

The grandfather is making a connection with his teen grandson like no other relationship he's ever had. As the grandfather repeats his grandson's answer, he's letting this young man know that he's listening to every word in his answer. And you'll also notice through this example that the answers take the relationship to a deeper level. It's called reflective listening, and it's a way that I've developed through the years to let a teen know of my interest in their words and of my desire to move to deeper levels in the relationship.

I know a young man named Mike who struggled at home. He often said to me that he had a tough time finding someone who would just listen to him. Mike was not a bad kid. He just wanted to have a relationship with someone who would show a bit of compassion and empathy as he wrestled with normal adolescent issues.

He thought and felt things a little more deeply as well. Mike struggled with a little bit of depression. He rejected my suggestion of going to see a counselor. "They're always trying to fix me instead of listening to what I have to say," Mike said.

In desperation, this young man got to the end of his rope, figuratively and literally. He tried to hang himself. Finally, that got the attention of those around him. He didn't die, but he did damage his spine to the point that he'll spend the rest of his life in a wheelchair. Mike told me that his unsuccessful attempt to kill himself was so that the people he loved would read the six-page letter he wrote describing what he was feeling and thinking all along. All Mike wanted was someone to listen. It almost cost his life.

Grandkids are dying for someone just to listen. Don't pay that awful price. Be the listening ear they need.

The fool speaks, the wise man listens.

—ETHIOPIAN PROVERB

Chapter 9

NAGGING AND LECTURING WORK LIKE FINGERS IN A DIKE

My dear brothers and sisters, take note of this: Everyone should

be quick to listen, slow to speak and slow to become angry.

JAMES 1:19 (NIV)

I think you know by now I tend to tell it like it is. So I'm warning you up front. This chapter may step on some grandparents' toes.

As the kids say today, "Sorry, not sorry."

It's important to talk about certain communication styles many grandparents employ. You used them when you were parents and continue to use them now as grandparents. I'm focusing on two styles in particular—nagging and lecturing. They don't work.

NAGGING AND LECTURING

Leave the nagging and lecturing to the parents to do in their children's early years. If you keep these bad communication habits when your grandkids become teens, I predict you will destroy your relationships.

Okay, I'm going to make some assumptions here. In most families, grandmothers do more of the nagging, while grandfathers have a propensity to lecture.

Grandmothers love teaching their grandkids. Watching little ones grow, develop, and begin verbal engagement is absolutely wonderful. Grandmas get in the habit of teaching. Kids through the age of twelve need to be taught. It's the right model. Teaching involves repetition, constant questions, continuous urging, and helping with appearance and behavior. Grandmothers desire the very best in the lives of their little grandchildren. Am I getting myself in trouble here?

Grandfathers love to transfer thoughts, opinions, and the lessons they've learned to their grandkids. But when grandchildren are young, grandfathers pretty much stay in *let's play* mode. When those little kids turn twelve or thirteen, grandfathers spring into action. Suddenly their grandchildren need to take more responsibility, start growing up, learn some lessons, and hear about the duties in life. This is the window of opportunity; time to gather their messages together and start lecturing.

One granddaughter I know described her grandfather as a know-it-all who never wanted to listen to anyone. "He might as well go into a room, look into the mirror, and have a conversation with himself. He needs no one else to talk to," she said.

Of course, I'm sure grandmas lecture at times, just as there are times when grandpas nag.

A Google search of the *Oxford English Dictionary* for the definition of the verb *nag* defines it as: *to annoy or irritate* (a person) *with persistent fault-finding or continuous urging.*[3]

The *Merriam-Webster Dictionary* defines *nagging* as: *to annoy* (someone) *by often complaining about his or her behavior, appearance, etc.; to annoy with repeated questions, requests, or orders.*[4]

Grandparents tend to communicate through repetition, which is needed before adolescence but must be transitioned away from when grandkids hit their teen years.

*A nagging wife—***grandparent** *[my insert]—is like the dripping of a leaky roof in a rainstorm. Stopping her is like trying to stop the wind. It's like trying to grab olive oil with your hand.* (PROVERBS 27:15–16, *NIRV*)

The nag annoys with repeated requests or orders that might sound such as these:
- "Did you remember what I told you?"
- "Did you remember today is your mother's birthday?"
- "Did you clean up after yourself?"
- "Do I need to repeat myself?"
- "Are you listening to me?"
- "Did you buy a Christmas gift for your brother?"
- "Did you take care of . . . ?"
- "Why isn't that done yet?"

The nag never stops. They wonder why they get responses such as these:
- "Okay, okay, I get it."
- "Stop! I understood you the first time."
- "I heard you the first time!"

- "No, I didn't hear you. I just wanted to hear you repeat it again." (Insert sarcasm here.)
- "You don't need to tell me again!"
- "I'll get on it when I have time!"
- "I'm not an idiot!"
- "You're not my mother!" (or father)

HOW YOU'RE COMING ACROSS

This is how teens think when someone continually reminds them of what to do, what to remember, or how to behave. Your granddaughter thinks you believe her to be incompetent and irresponsible. Your grandson thinks you're telling him he can't be trusted to complete a project. Your grandchildren will get the message that you think they are inadequate, immature, and ignorant. That's what they hear. But they're still learning.

I truly believe there is one role for the parents and a different but complementary role for grandparents. In the best of cases. When parents try to take over the role of a grandparent, they forget what their role needs to be in the life of their child. And when a grandparent reaches out of bounds and tries to be the parent, the children miss out on an important relationship unique to the one with their grandparents.

Nagging eliminates influence. Nagging at teens also inspires rebellion. The more you nag, the less they listen. If nagging becomes the norm, they will eventually write you off.

One young man described his grandmother as one who always felt the need to focus on the negative. She demeaned her grandkids. But her presentation came out all wrong. Her family expected her indictments of them whenever they saw her coming, so they eventually just wrote her off. No one missed her when she passed.

Teens need grandparents to focus on them, but not only on the parts of them that need improvement. Put your emphasis on the interests of your grandchildren. Extend grace, not condemnation. Nagging focuses on what they are not doing. Instead, focus on the good things they are doing.

I've nagged you long enough.

Truth be told, your grandkids probably hate your lectures. They love your stories but can't stand your lectures. Conversations and discussions are two-way streets. No one's eyes should glaze over. Aim for dialogues, not monologues, with your grandchildren.

I know you want to transfer your sage advice before you are gone so your grandchildren's world will get better and they won't suffer the consequences as you did. That's a great goal, but it needs to be met over time. Make sure you move from lectures to discussions.

Try Something Different

Be brief. I prefer a half-dozen ten-minute discussions to one hour-long one. While I wish we could sit down for hours and talk, most teens aren't accustomed to sitting still and being attentive that long. Most have not been trained to be able to do so. When teens walk away from me, I want them to know I was interested in what they had to say, kept the conversation brief so they'd want to talk again, and believe we can think differently and still have great connecting conversations.

Take advantage of the times they approach you. My granddaughter recently came to me and asked if she could work for me. She wanted to make some gas money for transportation. My response was, "Sure. Come talk to me and tell me what you want." When she came over, I just said, "Hey, let's talk about your need for a job."

As we sat down, I asked a different question. "Do you think you'll drink alcohol when you're in college?" I asked. I asked the question casually, and she responded easily. We talked for a bit, and I was able to let her know how much I appreciate her opinions. I didn't share mine. After ten minutes of talk, I transitioned the discussion to what she really came over for.

Take advantage of the times your grandchildren come to you and want something. Turn them into opportunities to have one of those short discussions that help you get to know them and the beliefs and values they embrace as their own. I learned years ago I'm not afraid to briefly discuss heavier topics when they want something from me. It may seem like a bit of a conversational manipulation on my part, but it is worth it for the sake of a deeper connection.

Here's a fun way to get interesting conversations going. Have an "All-Text Thursday (or any day) Dinner." What in the world is that? It goes like this. Have your grandkids over to eat and make sure everyone has a smartphone capable of texting. Set up a group text with everyone at the table. Let everyone know via group text that all conversation (I mean every word) will be communicated through texting. No talking. Not a peep out of anyone.

Text everyone when it's time to eat dinner. As all come to the table, have a prayer already written to be texted to everyone. Send the prayer. Then text "Amen." As you hear the notification *dings* around the table, start texting for the potatoes. Next, text for someone to pass the meat. Then text for the vegetables. Have fun texting as the only form of communication for the night. Text if someone can get more tea or water for the meal. Text if someone can bring in dessert. Text and ask if all are enjoying the meal.

Then text the following question, "Hey, what's one thing you'd like to see different in your life?" Remember, you'll get a wide variety of responses depending on the ages of your grandchildren. But it's a different way to pry open the doors of their hearts and minds. Kids respond frankly via text. They say things they wouldn't say face-to-face. So this may be a way to get them to let their guard down and let you in more. You may be surprised at their answers.

Over time, after a couple of All-Text Thursdays, ask a question that dives a little deeper into their hearts. Ask them, "Have you ever been depressed?" or "Do you know anyone who has thought about suicide?" or "What has been the hardest time of your life?"

Don't nag. Don't lecture. Listen to their hearts. In time, they'll begin to ask you questions.

Instead of Open-Ended Questions, Have Open-Ended Discussions

When I meet people on an airplane, I find sometimes it's easier to talk to strangers than people I've known for years. Interesting, eh? Maybe it's because all things are new. It's interesting to find out about their lives, and I'm all ears to hear their stories. Perhaps trying this technique with your grandchildren would let them know that you are all ears about them. Sit down next to a grandchild sometime, extend your hand for a shake, and introduce yourself. Say something like, "Hi, I'm your grandpa. What's your name?" Act like you don't know where they're from, where they go to school, or anything about them. See what they have to share.

Hey, kids love to talk about themselves. Give them the opportunity. Eventually they'll circle back and show more interest in you because you show interest in them.

Keep asking questions and just wait for it. Wait for that magical moment when they ask that first question of importance. They'll eventually start asking you more questions that will lead to the discussions you long to have.

Picture it like this: you're on one side of the door of your grand-children's hearts. They're on the other. Your words push on the door trying to open it. If you nag, the door won't budge. If you insist on making the relationship go your way, it's like pushing the door into their faces. Ouch! But over time you'll find you weren't supposed to be pushing the door. You'll find out that you were supposed to be letting the door be pushed from the other side. And with words of love and encouragement, the door will be pushed from the other side. And it will swing open.

If you don't have a good answer to their questions or you're not ready to share one, end your discussion with any of these comments to keep the conversation open-ended and ongoing. You can pick it up the next day or the next time you're able to talk together.

- "I need to think about that before I answer."
- "You know, I'm not sure, but I'll find out and circle back with you."
- "I don't know. Can I get back with you?"

- "Wow, that's a tough one. I'm not sure. What do you think?"
- "Hey, I'm interested in your comments about this. Can we come back to it later?"
- "Man, that's a great question. I need some time to come up with a good answer."

A string of conversations that happens over a period of time has much more impact than one big conversation that tries to answer it all.

Quit Interrupting

I've talked of it before. The greatest barrier to effective conversation is interrupting. It's just rude. It comes across as arrogance. The second the interruption happens, a message is sent to your grandchild that clearly states your thoughts are much more important than what he has to say. Here are a couple of scriptures to keep you from interrupting, verses that share the wisdom in listening first before answering.

> *Everyone should be quick to listen, slow to speak and slow to become angry.* (JAMES 1:19)
> *Let people finish speaking before you try to answer them. That way you will not embarrass yourself and look foolish.* (PROVERBS 18:13, ERV)

So let them speak. Sure, they'll stumble over words, repeat themselves, and say stupid things. Nine times out of ten you can guess what their next words will be. You might even feel bored. Still, you need to pay attention. Above all, you want your grandchildren to feel honored and respected because you give them your full attention when you listen.

Grandma and Grandpa, you don't want your grandkids to think of you as lecturing old nags. If they put you in that category, they are likely to treat you like one—an old nag horse that will be put out to pasture, fed, and tolerated, but not paid much attention. I don't think that's what you desire in your relationships with your grandkids.

Chapter 10

EVERYONE'S ARGUMENT DOESN'T NEED ARGUING

Even fools are thought wise if they keep silent,

and discerning if they hold their tongues.

PROVERBS 17:28 (NIV)

We live in a world where people love to argue. It's everywhere! Turn on any news channel and you hear arguing. There are TV programs where the focus of interaction is to do nothing but argue. Newscasters love a good argument because it creates good stories. Teens argue back and forth on social sites. Adults argue their points of view in postings and blogs. Politicians spend their lives arguing for this or against that, and groups of people argue for their rights and their longing to be heard.

Now we're not talking about nagging; we're not talking about giving an ear; we're headed into something entirely different. Arguing. Arguing flourishes today because people aren't listening to one another. When the art of listening disappears, people choose to quarrel, disagree, squabble, bicker, fight, wrangle, dispute, and feud. It's been that way since the beginning of time. The difference today is we have more tools and electronic gadgets to use to argue. Technology makes arguments more readily available, and the capacity for not listening a little easier.

One group sees things one way, and another sees it a different way. There is something inherent in us to want other people to agree with us. We feel valued when we are in accord with one another. In the same way, we feel less valued when others do not agree with us.

The fight to express diverging or opposite views, usually in a heated exchange, is self-focused. If we are intent on persuading others to share our views at all costs, we are self-centered. It's a one-way street—our way or the highway. When two or more people engage in conversation in this manner, it's nothing but a fight. It's all *me first* thinking, with a goal of the meeting of personal needs rather than the needs of anyone else in the conversation. How does that kind of talk line up with this scripture?

> *Don't have anything to do with foolish and stupid* arguments, *because you know they produce quarrels. And the Lord's servant must not be quarrelsome but must be kind to everyone, able to teach, not resentful.* (2 TIMOTHY 2:23–24, *emphasis added*)

NOT EVERY ARGUMENT
NEEDS TO BE ARGUED

Some arguments sound good but are steeped in issues that violate everything you believe and hold to be true. Even so, the people making those arguments deserve to be heard. Why? Because all people need to feel valued, known, and heard or they won't be able to trust and listen to any other view. It may take everything you've got not to hotly defend biblically based beliefs you hold dear, especially when you feel attacked. However, here's where your gentle answer can turn away anger. Your reasoned responses, delivered in ways that honor and respect the other person, allow them to hear a different belief without going on the defensive.

In a culture where arguments are the norm and resolutions are rarely achieved, I suggest arguing isn't the best way to influence. Matter of fact, arguing with teens many times just solidifies their position and justifies their viewpoint.

If you're a grandparent of teens, remember this: Not every argument needs to be argued.

I was with a fellow a few months ago who has been receiving quite a bit of criticism about his views on homosexuality. Adamantly opposed to the homosexual lifestyle, he has been bashed and bruised by some media outlets. Others applauded him for his stance and willingness to *speak the truth*. He told me stories of what people are saying about him, revealed threats that have been thrown his way, and showed me how vicious people's responses have been to him.

After listening to what had been happening to him because he stood up for what he believes in, I just sat. He then asked what I thought. Instead of answering right away, I first asked him, "Are you looking for an answer or my opinion?" He opened the door.

I said, "Dude, you need to shut up. You're only going to get bashed, and you may be worsening the issue, not helping."

He was shocked and replied, "Well, someone's got to stand in the gap!"

I responded, "No, not really. If a gentle answer turns away wrath, then I wonder why your answer is not doing that."

It's because his message wasn't being heard as *gentle*. It came across abrasive, in fact. He might have done better to abide by these words.

> *Do not give what is holy to the dogs; nor cast your pearls before swine, lest they trample them under their feet, and turn and tear you in pieces.* (MATTHEW 7:6, NKJV)

That's exactly what was happening to him. He based his beliefs on what is holy. The Bible can be seen as his pearls here. But casting them widely into a culture that largely doesn't care to hear them didn't work.

One tool you might use to decide whether to speak is to ask yourself this question first. *Does what I am about to say, HEAL?* What I mean by that is this acronym is, does it **H**elp? Does it **E**ncourage? Does it **A**ffirm? Is it **L**oving? The young man I was speaking to might have the right beliefs, but his comments evidently were not interpreted as helpful, encouraging, affirming, and loving. As such, they did not HEAL. While well-meaning, they caused more division, as seen in the directly opposing comments and backlash he received.

I find as I get older, I don't want to argue anymore. If someone says something contrary to what I believe, I just let them think what they want and leave it alone. That doesn't mean I don't defend my beliefs if I am directly asked. It just means I don't butt in where I'm not invited. It also means I think my beliefs stand on their own. I don't think I have to defend them. Why? Because I will win more people with my love and genuine caring for their hearts than I will be known as a big mouth.

If people in this culture aren't listening, your arguments for your beliefs won't be heard. When you spend your time and efforts building relationships instead of a platform, then you can speak of your beliefs when invited to within those close relationships. That's when hearts, spirits, and lives are changed. I love Jesus because He first loved me.

Until there is a place of safe established relationships where people will listen and allow others to be heard, there's no use in throwing your pearls before swine. You got to know when to hold them, know when to fold them, know when to walk away, and know when to run. That's called wisdom.

I DON'T WANT TO FIGHT THEM

At any given time, I live with sixty high school kids from all over the country. They are great kids with great parents who are struggling with some pretty substantial issues and behaviors. The teens need a place away from home to address some of the things going wrong in their lives, so they come to Heartlight for a year. We have faced about anything you can think of that has to deal with inappropriate behavior, wrong thinking, poor choices, and various lifestyles and backgrounds.

Parents send their kids to us in hopes we can help their teen and give the parents direction as to how to handle their child differently. Many families also want us to solve their extended family problems that have been around for years. That isn't our battle in the war for their teen's heart and life.

Under the banners of standing for what's right, seeking justice, and fighting the good fight, many come to a point where anything opposed to what they believe is grounds for battle. At the very least, many people seem to want to grapple until others understand where they stand.

Many grandparents go to sleep at night feeling they did what is right in the eyes of the Lord when they stood up against their grand-kids. They mistakenly believe it's a good thing when they let their teen grandchildren know what is right and what is wrong. Many don't realize what they are truly doing is alienating their grandkids, not only from themselves but also often from the truths they are trying to communicate. Be careful not to wield a verbal sword and cut your grandkids down and keep them from being positively influenced by you in the future.

Doing what is right in the eyes of the Lord doesn't mean you have to argue anything contrary to scripture. Please hear me carefully here. You should honor God in all that you do. I'm not encouraging you to give up your beliefs for the sake of a better relationship with your grandchild. I am encouraging more forward thinking. Think through the impact of what you might argue for or against. Then determine whether the argument will deepen your special relationship. You both need a close and loving bond. Will your stance threaten that? If it will, then don't lose your position over an argument that will never be settled peacefully.

I want to be a lifter of burdens for my grandkids, not one who places more on them.

By the time they are teens, they know the difference between right and wrong. They know what scripture has to say about certain issues. Their parents have taught them things they have to sort and figure out for themselves. As a grandparent, I want to help them do that.

It's not my role to fight with them. It's my role to be a sounding board for them. They talk; I listen. I ask if they want input. If they say no, I honor that. When they make good choices, I rejoice with them. When they make wrong turns, I hurt with them and for them.

That's tough sometimes. I'll admit it. I'm a Texan, a typical Texan who doesn't mind standing up for what is right or defending my beliefs. I've even had times when I've encouraged a good fight with a comment like, "Bring it on!" However, I draw a line in the sand before I go to battle with my grandkids. I do not want a quick win of a battle that turns into the heartbreaking loss of the war for their love, trust, and special relationship with me.

LIVING IN A DIFFERENT WORLD

Grandkids live in a different world today where differing views are prevalent. How they see issues and how we grandparents see them may be as different as night and day.

Recently I heard from a young lady who is a wonderful friend. However, she wanted to have a conversation with me that had been brewing in her for some time. She wanted to let me know she'd moved in with a girl she had fallen in love with. She said, "I'm gay. I love Jesus, and I know that He loves me. I've had to come to terms with that." You know, for some those are fighting words.

Her comments challenged my thinking and beliefs. Because we have developed a trusted relationship over time, I could have asked her any of the following questions. *How can you think that way? What would Jesus say about your comments? How can you justify what the Bible says about homosexuality?*

I didn't ask any of those things. I chose to say only, "Sweetheart, I want you to know this. There's nothing you can do to make me love you more, and there's nothing you can do to make me love you less." In a moment I decided the most important way to engage with this dear friend was to communicate a love for our relationship. I let her know I love her dearly. I chose not to correct her. I believe my role is to love. Let the conviction of the Holy Spirit do the correcting. Those life choices, the lifestyle she is embracing, are between her and God.

Saddleback Church Pastor Rick Warren, the author of the best-selling book *The Purpose Driven Life*, once stated,

> Our culture has accepted two huge lies. The first is that if you disagree with someone's lifestyle, you must fear or hate them. The second is that to love someone means you agree with every-thing they believe or do. Both are nonsense. You don't have to compromise convictions to be compassionate.[5]

Don't compromise your convictions. But be sure to create a place of discussion where differences of opinion are allowed. Those are tough places for your grandkids to find. Bring compassion and open up communication. Jesus said, "Come to me and I will give you rest" (see Matthew 11:28). Be like Jesus to your grandkids. Offer them a place of safety and rest, not argument and rejection. If you do, when life gets too tough to handle, they'll run to you.

Chapter 11

QUIT CORRECTING AND START CONNECTING

Let us think of ways to motivate one another to

acts of love and good works.

Hebrews 10:24 (NLT)

*I*f I spend all my time correcting everything wrong with the kids living with us at Heartlight, I wouldn't have any time left for the relationships God desires for me to have with them. No one can get everything right all the time.

You may see a lot of things wrong with your grandkids. They may get on your last nerves and bring out all your pet peeves. Does any of this sound familiar? They make messes, and we have to clean up after them. Rarely do they help with dishes. They spend too much time on their phones. They play too many stupid games on their iPads and computers. They never wash the sheets. They track in dirt and leave dirty towels lying around. They dig through my stuff and use whatever they want without asking.

My grandkids' sloppiness may feel like bad manners to me, but do I correct them? Nope. They need to be connected, not corrected.

In my seminars for parents of teenagers, I somewhat jokingly tell parents to correct teens only on Mondays, Wednesdays, and Fridays. Give them a break from a culture that is always telling them what they do wrong, how they can do it better, and what they need to do differently next time. I encourage parents to correct, but also to give breaks from correction. See, correction may change surface behavior. Connecting changes the heart.

I encourage grandparents not to correct at all. Am I crazy? Sure, there are things that bug me about my grandkids. However, short of violating the hard-and-fast rules Jan and I have for our home (listed in chapter 20), we don't correct the grandkids when they visit. Why? Because correction is their parents' job. I believe it's a better strategy for grandparents to give their grandkids a break. Focus on connection with them in ways that build your special relationship. Eventually they'll do better about their messes because they care about you. (It may take years. Be patient.)

If your grandson puts in a good day's work mowing your yard, and the first thing you notice is the patch of grass he missed, I guarantee he won't be back to mow again if he can help it. Even if they are true, refrain from comments that his performance wasn't near as good as you hoped, that he mowed it all wrong, or that he didn't quite finish what he started. Those complaints turn his willingness to help into failure. He wasn't good enough. He didn't meet your exacting expectations.

You could lose a lifetime of influence in a moment of correction. It's not worth it.

If a granddaughter comes over and you don't think she is properly dressed, I'd encourage you to stay away from trying to improve her appearance. Button your lips and don't deliver a message on being modest. If she feels criticized or corrected, she may not be back.

UNDERSTANDING THEIR BEHAVIOR

I deal with kids who are struggling, and the tendency for parents is to try to manage their child's behavior. In some ways, parents have to do that. Their children are their responsibility. But correcting behavior can put a wedge between parents and kids that keeps them from getting to the heart of the real issues that are driving the inappropriate actions.

Behavior is goal oriented. Your grandchild reacts and responds for a reason. There is a method to her madness. There is intention in your grandson's bad behavior. Your grandkids' behaviors are visible expressions of the invisible issues within. A wise grandparent will see beyond the behavior and engage in a way that speaks to their hearts. Grandparents should not try to manage grandchildren's actions.

You can help with heart issues by asking questions that help them get to the root of their conduct. If you've done a good job creating a place of rest and a haven of wisdom, grandkids can feel safe sharing what is really going on. This gives you a chance to speak to their deeper internal struggles.

Here are some questions you can ask to get beyond behavior and target the heart:
- Hey, Bud, tell me what's really going on?
- Sweetie, I can see that there's a little bit of conflict. Anything I can help with?
- Tell me, what's driving the stuff your parents shared with me?

- Do you think the behavior I see might be connected to something I don't see? What am I not seeing?
- If you could change one thing in your life at the snap of your fingers, what would that be?
- Man, that sounds like a mess. Is there any way I can help in all of this?
- Help me understand what you're thinking. I'm a little confused.
- Hey, how's life in the dark hole? Maybe I can help you find a way out.
- Your words say one thing, but I feel like your behavior says something completely different. Help me identify the difference.

Asking the right question at the right time is an amazing way of opening the door to your grandchild's heart, especially when their answer doesn't invoke a consequence or a form of discipline.

SPEAKING THE LANGUAGE THAT TOUCHES THEIR HEARTS

In 1995, Dr. Gary Chapman wrote a wonderful marriage book called *The Five Love Languages: How to Express Heartfelt Commitment to Your Mate.* This book continues to hit the bestseller lists more than twenty years since it was first published. It's that good. It contains simple truths that are so profound. The book outlines five ways to express and experience love, which Chapman calls *love languages.* These five languages are the giving of gifts, quality time, words of affirmation, acts of service, and physical touch.

Many parents and grandparents have applied the same love language tests to their teens, thinking if they learn how their child (grandchild) receives love, they can better meet their needs.

Not long ago, I was a guest on Gary's *Building Relationships* radio program. I remember asking him if he thought there were more than five love languages. I don't remember his answer, but it did get me thinking.

Years ago we thought there were just nine planets in our solar system. That's what I learned growing up. As young students, we all learned their names by heart and many made mobiles out of coat hangers and Styrofoam balls painted various colors. We made posters and shoebox dioramas of our massive solar system for science projects through my junior high school years.

The great mystery of our time was the planet Pluto that was discovered in 1930. Scientists argued for years over whether it's a planet or not.

Then something happened in the early 1990s. The first extra-solar planet was discovered, a planet outside of our solar system that orbits a star. What did experts name it? *51 Pegasi b*. It was discovered the same year Gary Chapman's book was published.

Do you want to know how many extra-solar planets have been discovered since that first one? Three thousand, four hundred, and ninety-eight. The number of planets is far beyond what we could have ever imagined. We thought there were just nine, and now we know of thirty-five hundred. Amazing, isn't it?

I thought if we believed for so long there were just nine planets (Pluto sometimes in, sometimes out), and now there are 3,498, there must be a possibility that when we thought there were just five love languages, there might be a couple more.

I knew there had to be other love languages because those written by Gary never really applied to me. I don't want more gifts because I've got too much stuff already. I don't want quality time because I don't have any more time to give.

Just because those love languages don't fit me doesn't mean they're not true. Of course, they are. I think I'm the odd duck here. How do I feel loved?

I spent the next few months thinking about what other love languages might be. Eventually, I came up with a few that touched my heart. I believe these apply to teens everywhere.

Here are two additional ways a grandparent can express love for the adolescent grandchild.

1. *Defend the ones you love. Show your loyalty.* A teen desires to know he is loved when all is well. He also wants to know he

is loved when things aren't so well, when peers and others turn against him for whatever reason, even if he's wrong. Your grandkids want to know that when others are against them, you will be for them, speak up for them if need be, and stand by their side. When you listen to them complain about relationships, don't take the other person's side, *even if your grandchild is wrong.* Over time, most issues will work themselves out and your grandchild will remember how you listened. Show them your loyalty, and they'll feel loved.

2. *An invitation to participate.* Most kids want to be invited to participate even though they might not attend whatever they've been invited to. I'm the same way. I hate to be left out; just don't expect me to show up when you extend the invitation. I think that I want to be included just as much as teens want to belong. They're desperate to know they are wanted. They want to fit in, long to be popular, desire to be admired. The hardest thing for any teen is to feel left out, excluded, or forgotten about. That's why they're on their phones so much. They don't want to miss anything.

When you defend a grandchild who has been offended, you open the door for a lifelong relationship.

When you invite your grandchildren to join you, you build a relationship.

They will not forget your loyalty or the time you spent with them.

WHEN THE CONNECTION JUST ISN'T HAPPENING

When connection isn't happening, the first thing you must do is ask them some questions.

The first question is this simple one: "What am I doing that is keeping us from connecting?" Flat out ask the question. Send it in a text. Tell your grandchild you'd like to talk about it at some point. Get to the real answer. It may be something you do. There may be one of your mannerisms that just bug them. It may be how you treat their friends. It may be something you are saying. They may be embarrassed by your comments. They may just think you're goofy.

Ask the question. The focus of the question is to see how you can get past whatever it is that is keeping them from making a connection with you. One of our girls at Heartlight came up to me at one of our family retreats and asked me if I would talk to her grandmother. She said, "Mark, would you talk to my grandmother and tell her and ask her to quit sending me scripture and all her words of encouragement? They make me feel judged, like she just wants to correct me all the time."

In this case, a positive, encouraging act done by a grandparent was interpreted as something different by the granddaughter. In time, this young lady will welcome her grandmother's words of encouragement, but for now, she wanted no part of them. The best thing for this grandmother would be to quit texting. The best of intentions can be perceived completely differently. Stop if you're getting in the way of the relationship.

Correction isn't one of the love languages. You can either choose to *correct* their behavior, which is a temporary fix or, you can *connect* for a lifetime.

What do you think your grandchildren really want?

– PART III –

YOU KNOW THEY'RE WATCHING YOU AND THAT AIN'T ALL BAD

Chapter 12

COMPLAINING RUINS RELATIONSHIPS, GRATEFULNESS DRAWS THEM IN

When you talk, don't say anything bad. But say the good things

that people need—whatever will help them grow stronger.

Then what you say will be a blessing to those who hear you.

EPHESIANS 4:29 (ERV)

As the years pass quicker and quicker, the unavoidable aging process appears. We can't help but notice the downward gravitational pull on our bodies. It's inevitable. It's foreseeable. It's certain. We're getting older. The inescapable reality of our fates is that one day we will be gone. What will remain are the memories of who we were. Most won't remember all the things we said, but they will remember how we *made them feel*. My prayer is that I never make anyone feel uncomfortable around me.

So I've made some choices.

THE CRANKS

Because I don't want to get fat, I work out to make sure I stay in shape the best I can. Because I love good health, I watch what I eat. Because I don't want to break anything, I watch the activities I engage in. Because I don't want two earfuls of hair, age spots all over my face, shriveled and damaged hands, and veins road mapping my nose, I choose dermatological procedures to keep that from happening.

I can control some choices I make in life for my health.

You know what I want more than anything else? I want to be a grandpa who is grateful for what and who I have in my life.

I know this for sure: My wife doesn't want to become a cranky old woman who rants and raves about everything. I can't imagine a Jan who expresses disappointment that life should have treated her better. I know my wife wants to be grateful and thankful for each day God gives her. She is.

These desires go hand-in-hand with the choices we make. Short of developing dementia or losing your physical health, you can choose the cranky and cantankerous. As long as you have your faculties, you have a choice. That choice determines whether your legacy is a positive one to be remembered or a negative one hopefully quickly forgotten.

I'm not sure people actually realize how they come across. I'm sure most folks prefer to be seen as good-natured. I haven't met anyone who truly wants family, friends, and strangers alike to avoid them. However, many grandparents don't know just how their grandkids see them. I interviewed a number of teens and asked them to tell me about their grandparents. Some of their answers were not complimentary. Most were just sad. Here's how they described some of their grandparents:

- Very bitter about everything.
- Full of disappointment.
- Argues about everything, is just looking for a fight.
- Has become crabby and disagreeable.
- Judgmental attitude toward everything.
- Opinionated, with outbursts full of gripes or criticisms.
- Complains about everything.
- Unreasonable, belligerent, and grouchy.
- Never shuts up.

With some degree of certainty, I'm pretty sure I've never met a grandparent who said, "You know, I sure would like to be like . . . ." any one of the statements I just listed. But it happens. When grandparents wonder why their grandkids don't want to be in their presence, it baffles me how many don't have a clue why they are being avoided.

ARE YOU AN OFFENSIVE COMPLAINER?

Here are a couple of things you can do to find out if you have become an offensive person who is to be avoided. Ask God to search your heart. Psalm 139:23–24 says,

Search me, God, and know my heart; test me and know my anxious thoughts. See if there is any offensive way in me, and lead me in the way everlasting.

You can pray for God to reveal what it is in you pushing your grandchildren away. It may be the very thing your spouse has said for years. You probably heard it from your kids when they lived in your home. Perhaps coworkers or bosses said it to you or about you.

This is what's on the line. Your relationships and your legacy hang in the balance here. It's time to deal with those unpleasant ways you've developed, so you can ensure your legacy is one to be remembered, not one to be quickly forgotten.

If you're afraid to ask your kids and grandkids how they see you, that's a good indicator you might have some areas to work on. Text them and try it. Pure and simple, you know kids will say things in texts they wouldn't say face-to-face. So ask them. Text them these questions, "What is it that makes you want to avoid me? What am I doing to push you away?"

If they text back, "You complain and gripe about everything," don't rush to justify. Accept their words, tell them thanks for sharing, and begin to change. Even at your age, you can make new habits, especially if the old ones are getting between you and your grandkids.

No one likes a complainer or grumbler, one who is discontent with his lot in life. Remember Philippians 2:14 from those old Sunday School lessons?

Do everything without complaining and arguing.

Most teens avoid constant complainers like the plague. They live in this culture of negativity all the time. If that's what they're going to get from grandma and grandpa, too, they will look elsewhere for their encouragement. There isn't any hope to be found in one who complains all the time.

I've met many people aging with a great deal of anger who are unhappy that life didn't turn out the way they hoped, and who are critical of folks and God because they feel abandoned. These whiners focus all their remaining energies on their losses and disappointments. These are reflected in their constant rants about how life would have been different if they were dealt a different hand.

I recently talked to a friend I've known for forty years. He began to speak of an incident that happened to him thirty-eight years ago. His discussion centered on how his life would have been so different if the pastor of the church he worked for almost four decades before had treated him differently. The discussion wasn't just a few sentences of disgust or disappointment. It lasted for forty-five minutes! This friend spent thirty-eight years rolling the scenario of disappointment around in his head, justifying his own loss, blaming someone else, and expressing his disappointment in life through his words and comments.

There are some battlefields where wars continue to be fought, even though the enemy is long gone. Those are the battlefields of your mind and your emotions. If you find yourself stuck, it will pour out on those around you. If you know there are things from the past you can't get past, it's time to get some help in the form of counseling and therapy. Even at your age, it is well worth the time and effort to become healthy. Then you can be a testimony of forgiveness, an example of healing and wholeness, and a beacon of hope to your grandchildren. It's never too late to repair and restore relationships.

GRATEFULNESS

Here's a hopeful story I offer to anyone who experienced disappointment and loss in their life.

I had high expectations for my dad in my life. As the years passed, I found I grew angrier and angrier with him. I expected him to be something he never was. I wanted him to give me things he never gave. Every time I saw him, I thought about how he hurt and upset me by failing to meet my expectations and give me opportunities to forge a deeper relationship with him.

I was angry for years, that quiet kind of anger that simmers continuously but never really boils over and burns anyone else. But I know it's there.

Then I had a dream. I dreamed I died and went to heaven. As I approached God, I noticed that my dad, the object of my years of anger, was standing next to Him as I was ushered into His presence. My anger boiled over. I was mad that Dad was standing next to God after continually disappointing me. I expressed my feelings to God, using some words I was shocked I would say to Him even in a dream.

God quickly stopped me. He answered with a short remark that changed my life. He said, "Mark, I want you to know something. I've been using your dad in your life to mold you into the person I wanted you to be." You know, that's all I needed to hear to understand why that happened in my life. The anger left.

What I thought was so bad was really a good thing. It's all about perspective. Because of my God-given new perspective, I'm not angry. Instead, I became extremely grateful for my circumstances. It's just sad that it took me until I was in my fifties before I realized what He was doing.

A heart full of gratefulness leaves no room for complaining. There's just something about a thankful person that is attractive and appealing.

It's as simple as this. Every time I cook a meal at our home when my granddaughter Macie comes over to eat, she always—I mean, always—says, "Thanks for dinner, Poppa." That is a simple comment, but it moves me every time. Her gratitude expressed in just those four words makes me want to cook every meal for her and make it the best it can be.

I know what I don't want to become in my older years. Ungrateful. I know exactly what I want for my grandchildren as they grow older—hope and gratefulness. I want them to be chock-full of hope and crammed with gratefulness for the life before them. I want them to know that whatever they face, they can get through it.

Regardless of your current circumstances, if you are grateful for who you are, what you have, and whom you have in your life, that's a legacy that will be talked about long after you're gone.

When you have hope, your grandchildren start to believe they can make it too. When they are overwhelmed, your joy and grateful heart can restore and refuel them. Because of what they see and hear from you, they believe they can move past tough situations. It also puts life into better perspective for teens; it tells them their hard days will pass. They will mess up, blow it, and let people down. Other people they know will mess it up too. Still, hope can prevail because they have seen you get through similar or worse situations.

Weeping may last through the night, but joy comes with the morning. (PSALM 30:5, *NLT*)

My dear friend Chelsea Cameron has been a guest on our radio show for years. Her words hit you strongly, and her message touches hearts as she shares her views on parenting. The most profound comment I've heard from her is the message she wants to communicate to her kids. "On our best of days, and our worst of days, I want you to know that our family is better because you are in it." Wow! What a message to convey to a tired and weary teen searching for significance and security. What hope to offer a kid who longs to belong to a family that will never quit on him!

Okay, grandparents, now you have a choice. Do you want to be a cantankerous and cranky? Or would you rather be grandparents full of hope, ones who are grateful for God's presence in their lives?

It's your choice. Choose wisely, my friends.

Chapter 13

CAN EVERYONE JUST LAUGH A LITTLE?

A cheerful heart is good medicine,

but a crushed spirit dries up the bones.

PROVERBS 17:22 (NIV)

When we started our *Parenting Today's Teens* radio program ten years ago, we traveled the country peddling our program to radio stations everywhere. We hoped they would pick it up and give us a chance to prove that the search was on for help and hope in raising teens. We relentlessly pursued these stations. Radio programmers did not want to take a chance. They had no idea who I was.

A BROADCAST OUT OF LEFT FIELD

To them, I came out of left field, starting a radio broadcast at age fifty-two. I had no previous history of recording or even an understanding of how to get people to carry a radio program. And they had no idea about how a program like ours would go over with their audience. When this guy in jeans and boots, with a mustache from the 1800s, strolled into radio stations, programmers had not seen anything like it before.

Nevertheless, some gave us a chance. Now many stations air our program, and it does well. We are thrilled to partner with so many wonderful radio stations throughout North America.

One organization asked if they could test the waters first. They wanted to see how I do while *on mic* (live on the air). They invited me to come in and do a drive-time program on a Tuesday morning from six to eight o'clock. The first hour would be me talking with the morning show host. The second hour would be me answering calls from the listening audience. Our radio team thought this would be a great opportunity to show who we were and give the radio station and their audience a taste of what we were all about. We decided to go.

The day before I was to go on-air with this station, a national scandal broke about a pastor. This pastor, who had been very anti-homosexual in his preaching and critical of the gay lifestyle, had made headlines once before when he got caught in a homosexual relationship exposed by his partner. A few years later, this pastor was in the national news again. The new story proclaimed the pastor "one hundred percent heterosexual" after going through counseling and therapy.

It was a big story for news sources when he was exposed; it was now bigger. So that was the setting the day before my trial run on this radio group, a group that was pretty conservative. Okay, it was very conservative.

We got to the studio early the next day; and our radio producer and good friend Roger looked at me and said, "Okay, Mark, now don't blow it!" The radio station's people all gathered to watch the guy with the mustache and to rely on their own instincts about carrying our program. I was on one side of the glass booth with the morning show host. Everyone else was on the other side sipping coffee.

The show began. For the first hour, I answered questions about teens and talked about the needs of adolescents. I told parents how they could counter the effects this contrary culture was having on their family. Everyone on the other side of the glass smiled, gave winks or nods at key moments, and told me between sessions they loved the interaction.

Then the second hour began. The host opened up the phone lines to take a few questions from the listening audience. Guess what the first question was? It was a young lady who said, "Mark, I have a question for you. Are you one hundred percent heterosexual?"

The folks on the other side of the glass slowly lowered their coffee cups in anticipation of my answer. Our producer Roger crossed his arms, then held his head in his hands. He rubbed his forehead and didn't even look up.

I answered, "You know, I don't think so." One would have thought I just stated that Billy Graham wasn't a Christian. Birds quit chirping, all traffic stopped, and the radio folks gasped when I said:

"You know, I don't think so," I repeated. "I think I'm ninety-five percent heterosexual, three percent metrosexual because I wear Tommy Bahama shirts occasionally, and two percent homosexual because I'd kiss Keith Urban if I had a chance." (Keith Urban is a country singer married to actress Nicole Kidman. I've been a fan for years.) I thought it was the perfect answer. Behind the smile on my face, I was belly laughing, thinking I just hit it out of the park. The radio guys did not agree.

Immediately, the live show switched to the weatherman sharing the forecast for the day. The next sound I heard was a loud rapping on the window and the producer saying, "You can't say that! YOU CAN'T SAY THAT!" Everybody got very quiet. All you could hear was the weather report droning on in the background. I thought this was a great defining moment for me to let them know who I am.

I stood up, looked through the glass at all the radio execs, and simply stated, arms stretched out, "If you guys don't lighten up, you'll never be able to discuss the hard issues with teens or their parents."

Great story, eh? Okay, I embellished a little, but you get my point. Right? You've got to lighten up. So many take everything so seriously that their intended message isn't accepted because of the sourpuss look on the messenger's face.

Our radio program is now one of their most popular weekend programs.

Throwing a Bigger Brick

I was speaking in Duck Dynasty Land last year and told this radio story to a church congregation. They roared with laughter. A seventy-five-year-old lady came up to thank me for my comments afterward. She said, "We haven't laughed like that in this church for twenty-five years!"

Then a thirty-year-old guy came up and said, "Mark, you know you can throw a bigger brick if it's wrapped in humor." Here was a young man who got it. My sentiments exactly.

Here are a couple of quotes from one of my heroes who evidently thinks like I do:

If you're not enjoying most of your day, if you've stopped having fun, you're missing more than you are contributing.[6]

How is your sense of humor? Are the times in which we live beginning to be reflected in your attitude, your face, and your outlook? Solomon says three things will occur when we have lost our sense of humor: a broken spirit, a lack of inner healing, and dried-up bones (Proverbs 15:13, 15; 17:22). What a barren portrait! Humor is not a sin. It is a God-given escape hatch, a safety valve. Being able to see the lighter side of life is a rare, vital virtue. (SWINDOLL, 220)[7]

I'm not encouraging laughing everything off. Good jokes do not make bad things good. Proverbs 25:10 (NLT) states,

Singing cheerful songs to a person with a heavy heart is like taking someone's coat in cold weather or pouring vinegar in a wound.

You have to be careful how you use humor but lightening a heavy moment with humor can make a hard truth easier to digest.

Lighten It Up

I encourage grandparents to lighten up a bit. Don't make everything so serious in your approach to your grandkids. You can talk about some very, very serious issues and still laugh in the middle of those hard discussions. Laughter lets them know your relationship is still intact, meaning without resentments, not bitter, and focused on the good, no matter how hard the conversation is. Hope is instilled, no matter how tough the situation, because you can still smile. Don't minimize the situation, but don't make it any bigger and heavier than it has to be.

Laughter is a form of worship. It lets everyone hear the confidence you have that God is still in control in the midst of whatever is happening. People hear your wisdom and acknowledge it when you don't have a frown on your face.

After living with thousands of teens, I know laughter is greatly needed in kids' lives. Their lives are so heavy. Their poor choices and consequences can be so grim. They need some innocent fun. There's nothing funny because they struggle with things that aren't fun. Truly, there's nothing funny about kids without new hope. Fun and laughter instill new hope.

When I finally hear laughter from a struggling teen, I know they are on a path to healing. Learning to laugh again becomes an essential part of discovering a renewed sense of hope.

LOOK FOR THE HUMOR IN SITUATIONS

Some of the greatest comedians spend their lives helping us look and laugh at ourselves. It's healthy. We're funny people. Just spend a little time at the mall or an airport, and you'll laugh when you see what a funny-looking and weird-acting species we are. When you laugh, remember people are laughing at you as much as you are laughing at them!

Do you think Jesus and the disciples ever had a good laugh? I mean, a hold-your-belly-crying-tears-can't-get-your-breath laugh that just couldn't stay contained? I think so. Here was a carpenter, a handful of fishermen, a tax collector, and the Lord only knows what everyone else did as an occupation (that's a joke!), and you don't think they laughed and told jokes?

Some of my funniest times in life have been when I'm with other fishermen. We tell stories, joke with one another, and have all kinds of fun catching our next meal. I bet you Jesus and the disciples were even told to keep it down a bit when they visited restaurants and stayed at inns.

There is a time for everything, including laughter.

> *A time to weep and a time to laugh, a time to mourn and a time to dance.* (ECCLESIASTES 3:4)

Look for Opportunities to Have a Good Belly Laugh

I recently had dinner with a family. They asked me to come by and spend the evening observing them. The parents wanted ideas to help change the declining relational atmosphere within their home. After an entire evening with the parents and three kids (two were teens), I asked the mom why it was so quiet around the table at dinner. Her response shocked me. She said, "We don't allow any laughter at the dinner table."

My comment shocked her. "You've got to be kidding me! That's horrible!" I said.

I never heard anyone come right out and say that. However, I've seen it implied in many different grandparents' homes. They're the ones where grandkids would choose to be elsewhere if they could.

I never limit laughter in my home. When my grandkids visit, I believe it's more important for them to have fun than to sit down and listen to my teaching, lessons, and diatribes about leading a successful and fruitful life. Why? Because if we have some fun and learn to laugh, the doors of their hearts will swing open. Their ears will open to hear what I need to share in the days ahead.

Here are some ways to add fun to your home:

- Watch a funny movie (one *they* think is funny).
- Grab an iPad and try to beat each other in a contest to find the funniest comedian on YouTube.
- Hold a joke night at dinner where everyone has to come to the table with a joke ready to be told. (Then give a prize of twenty dollars for the best joke.)
- Sit around the fireplace and tell the funniest stories you've ever heard.
- Spend time jokingly commenting on past events. Laugh about people's responses.

I like this quote:

I have not seen anyone dying of laughter, but I know millions who are dying because they are not laughing.[8]

Tell a Few Jokes and Give Yourself Permission to Laugh

One of the most serious men I've ever met makes sure he tells no fewer than three jokes when you are in his presence. It's become his trademark. And he tells the best jokes. Really. No one has an excuse for not being able to find good jokes for any age, as there are millions on the internet. Why not greet your grandkids at the door with a joke, saying, "Here, I got a good one for you!"

Give yourself permission not to be so serious all the time. Lighten up a little. Exaggerate your stories a bit to get a good response. Tell a joke to add some humor. Make fun of yourself, so your grandkids know you can have fun as much as the next guy. Laugh at your own mistakes so your grandkids will know you'll laugh at some of theirs.

Laughter is something that comes from within, reflecting an inner peace and the humility to let go and have a good chuckle.

Hey, put a smile back on your face. It's contagious.

Chapter 14

YOU'RE KIDDING ME—YOU WANT ME TO DO WHAT?

So we fix our eyes not on what is seen, but on what is unseen,

since what is seen is temporary, but what is unseen is eternal.

2 CORINTHIANS 4:18 (NIV)

Jan and I found a place of rest in a little town called San José del Cabo, located on the peninsula of Baja, California. We retreat there quite a bit to rest, write, and take a break from my crazy speaking engagements.

Last August we left our home to go to our little airport in Longview, Texas, on our way to San José del Cabo. We reached the airport at 4:30 p.m. and pulled my truck up to the front door to unload our bags. It's a tiny airport with only one gate to depart and arrive, and only two flights a day. I jumped out of the car to help unload our bags and ran in to get us all checked in.

In the process of checking in, they found that Jan's bags were overweight. That was no surprise to me, as the way Jan packs her belongings looks more like we're moving to Mexico than just visiting for a week. It took us twenty minutes to get it all straightened out, making sure we were within weight limits. The baggage was then sent off to be loaded onto the plane. The flight was already boarding, so we hurried through security, got on the plane, and flew to Dallas to await our next flight.

When we got to Dallas, we were told the next leg of our trip was delayed for four hours because of weather. We ate dinner, walked around a bit, and sat and waited to board the plane for our retreat to Mexico. As we finally got on the plane at midnight, now eight hours after the first leg began, I remembered something. The minute I stepped on the plane, I looked at Jan and said, "I left the truck running out in front of the airport in Longview." I never went back outside and parked it! I couldn't believe it. I had become so consumed with getting on the plane and getting through security that I forgot about my truck.

The flight attendant next to me heard my comment and decided to announce it to the whole plane. Everyone laughed at my forgetfulness. I quickly sat down and got on my phone amidst the chuckles and comments. I quickly called my daughter, hoping she could run to the airport and get my truck.

"Hey, Melissa, sorry to wake you up," I said.

"Are you guys in Mexico yet?" she replied.

"No, we were delayed a bit and just now got on the plane out of Dallas. I called because I need you to do something. I need you to go to the airport and get my truck."

I could tell she wasn't really excited about getting out of bed at midnight to help me when she said, "Sure, but why?"

"Your *mom* left the truck running in front of the airport," I replied. "Okay, I did it. But if Jan's bags hadn't been overweight, I would have remembered to go park it."

What is the moral of my story? Many times, in pursuit of what we think is *important* (of great significance), we forget about that which is most *valuable* and are of considerable importance and great worth).

For the sake of this chapter, let me clarify that what is *important* is usually focused on the here and now, and what is *valuable* has to do with that which will retain future value.

There are many things you wake up to each day that you think are important to complete or finish. Those important and much-needed tasks to complete nag at you until they are finished. They have an amazing way of eating up time, energy, and resources. The same time, energy, and resources could be expended to complete things that are more valuable and longer lasting.

WHAT IS VALUABLE TRADED FOR WHAT IS URGENT

Call it the tyranny of the urgent or exchanging what is valuable for what is urgent. Important things may be easier or screaming to be handled quickly. The reality is that many important matters take away opportunities for some pretty valuable intentions.

You may think it important to play golf, mow the yard, or spend the weekend working around the house, but what may be more valuable is hanging out with a granddaughter who just broke up with a boyfriend. And listening. That golf course will always be there and that grass will always keep growing, but your granddaughter will one day move away.

You may think it important to do your own thing, but what may be more valuable is being with your grandson and creating some memories. Your stuff can wait.

You may think it important to go fishing with your buddies, but what may be more valuable is taking a grandchild fishing so you all can spend some time together. Your time with your grandchild can change his life, and it's doubtful your buddy's life will change much because you hung out on a boat.

You may think it important to complete your project, but it may be more valuable to get that ice cream with a grandson or granddaughter who just needs some hang time with Grandma or Grandpa.

Maybe baking those cookies with a granddaughter is the very thing that saves her life . . . *seriously*! If you don't think so, then you don't understand the power you possess as a grandparent to bring hope to any situation.

What is the most valuable thing you can do for a grandchild? Invest your time. Invest your money. Invest your heart. That's what it will cost you. It's a big price, but the rewards for your involvement will return to you a hundred-fold in the way your family views you now and how they will remember you later.

Here's what I think is valuable in the lives of your grandchildren and worthy of your provision.

A LISTENING EAR

Everyone needs a valued listener, and your grandkids are no exception. Think about it. Who do they have that will really sit down, listen, and give them a place to vent and spew, complain, and criticize?

A young lady made a hurtful comment to me one day. She got in trouble for being disrespectful to some of our Heartlight staff. I merely said, "Want to hear some advice to get out of this mess?" I thought she would say, "Sure!" or "Yes, please tell me what I need to do," or "I would love to hear what you have to say." Those weren't her comments. She said, "Why would I listen to you? You don't even know who I am!"

She was teaching me once again a lesson I've heard many, many times before. You can't just listen for the sake of listening. Listening includes a heartfelt desire to get to know the person you're listening to or they will smell a rat a mile away. The purpose of listening is to understand. Grandkids know when you have an interest in their lives and want to hear all about them, and when you're just listening because that's what a good grandparent is supposed to do.

Grandkids want to be heard by someone who has an interest in them. You can be that person. That's more than important. If you want to know to know what is valuable, it is listening. Yes, that's what I want you to do.

Access to Wise Counsel

Sometimes grandkids need to vent to let out their frustrations. They must vent to someone who will keep private their stupid comments and absurd accusations. They know they're being ridiculous. They're just mad, and they want to get that anger out. You can be a safe place where they can let off some of their steam without scolding or making fun of what they say. You'll know when they want to rant. They get quiet, appear consumed by their own thoughts rather than what others are saying, and can't seem to "take things in" until they can "get things out." They have a need to "spew," and you can be that safe place for them to express their emotions.

Now, if a grandchild's comments are a violation of parents' rules or reflect a potentially damaging situation, then you need to share their rant with their parents. Make sure your grandchild knows that's the action you're going to take. But for the most part, a listening ear is all that is needed to calm your teen grandkids down when life throws them a curveball.

Give them time to speak what is on their hearts or stuck in their heads, and they'll either come to some resolution or ask you a question to help them get to one. When you have been this funnel of frustration a number of times, you'll begin to earn the right to be heard in the deeper, harder issues. I call those *decision-discussions* where they genuinely want to know what you think so they can come to a decision.

Typical teens learn from their own experiences. Wise teens learn from the experiences of others. Teens can't become wise if they don't have those others they can trust. Grandparents are in the perfect position to help their teens gain wisdom from their experiences. The grandparent with the listening ear can move a grandchild to a deeper level where they know there is always available understanding, compassionate listening, and healthy processing of their emotional turmoil.

Affirmation of Who They Are

The way you listen probably sends a greater message of hope than any words out of your mouth. Just as you know when someone is preoccupied with some other matter when you are talking, your grandchild knows the same. Any hint of distraction or disinterest will force your grandchild to search for another sympathetic listening ear. Make sure you give your undivided attention when you sit and listen. Create an atmosphere where you won't be interrupted.

I usually pick a restaurant I know will be quiet. My grandkids know that when I want to sit down and talk with them, we're going to a quiet place and we're going to sit in the back where interruptions are minimal. I plan it that way, and they expect it. I want them to know they are the most important things in my life when I sit down and open my ear to their hearts.

If you're like most granddads, you want to fix any problem they talk about. If you're like most grandmoms, you might want to give ten answers to their problem with personal scenarios for each. Many times all grandchildren need is someone to listen.

- Someone to listen without commenting unless asked.
- Someone to hear the frustration without telling them they're wrong.
- Someone to understand while not correcting how they're communicating.
- Someone to be satisfied with their comments without telling them how to say it better.

I encourage you not to try to fix or solve their issues. Just convey hope and tell them how special they are. Remind them of who they are whenever they forget.

You don't have to have an eloquent array of words. Just make them feel they are just as important to you now, sitting across from you in a discussion, as they were the day you first held them in your arms. Assure them they continue to be a blessing to your family, as they were the day they came into this world. Help them remember those who love them, rely on them, and with whom they have some very special and exceptional relationships. Make your teen grandkids feel valued.

Changing from Chalkboard Truth to Practical Application

One of the most valuable roles a grandparent plays in the lives of their grandchildren is helping them take the theoretical truths they have learned through their formative years and apply them in practical ways. This can be one of the most challenging, but rewarding, aspects of grandparenting. When they participate in this awakening, Grandma and Grandpa get to have an amazing impact on the hearts of their grandkids.

Here's an example. Most grandkids have heard Romans 8:28, "And we know that in all things God works for the good of those who love him, who have been called according to his purpose." They've heard it a million times, right? In one sense, it is theoretical truth for them until there comes a time for practical application.

That happens with a loss or a quick turn of events that changes the direction of a family. It might be a disaster, a catastrophe, or a hard-to-understand act of violence. It might even be a personal failure. In these situations, grandchildren need the wisdom of their grandparents to help them understand and comprehend what that particular scripture really means.

This transition of truth to an application isn't just accepted. It is transferred. It's something valuable that can only be done by a select few in a family. It's helping them balance what they know to be true with the way they feel. That's even more than valuable—it's invaluable.

THE BIGGER-PICTURE PERSPECTIVE

Help with the Puzzle of Life

Ever put together one of those thousand-piece puzzles you spread out over a table, and all gather around doing their part? It's funny to me that these usually take place at family events. The process pretty much reflects God's piecing together His masterpiece through all the family members putting together their conglomeration of jagged parts.

The borders go down first and then the rest of the pieces follow. Everyone usually selects a part of the puzzle and begins their work. They search and try to make the pieces fit, just like in life. You can usually hear the following comments from grandkids:

This piece doesn't fit.
There are some pieces missing.
I don't get how this is going to look.
These just don't go together.
I'm getting worn out.
This is taking so much time.

Wise grandparents keep folks (grandkids and all) on course by responding with the following:

This is how it fits together.
Take your time; there's no hurry.
Let's look at the bigger picture.
Each piece is important.
The dark pieces are just as needed as the brighter pieces.
Keep going. It's coming together.

The Colors of the Puzzle

Throughout the process, wise grandparents explain how it takes all colors to bring about the majesty of this masterpiece (just like life). How it takes time to get things right (just like life). How the dark pieces make the brighter pieces come to life (just like life). See my point? Helping grandkids put together a jigsaw puzzle is a lot like helping them put together the pieces of their lives. When you help them see and understand the similarities? That's invaluable.

Wise grandparents sacrifice the important things of today for the more valuable stuff of the future. That's what they do best. Oh, and about my truck? Yes, it ran for eight hours at the airport that night. The door was partway open and the radio playing. That's how small our airport is. Fortunately for me, my focus on the important didn't cost me what was more valuable. Putting your focus on your awesome grandkids? That's invaluable.

Chapter 15

THEY'RE WATCHING OUT OF THE CORNERS OF THEIR EYES

Let us not love with words or speech but with actions and in truth.

1 JOHN 3:18 (NIV)

"Actions speak louder than words."

"It's not what you say; it's what you do."

"I can't hear what you're saying because your actions are speaking too loud."

You've heard these sayings before, I know. You can't live as long as we all have without finding some placard or post that encourages integrity and promotes truthfulness.

You will be known to your grandkids by what you do, not what you say you will do.

The question to answer would be, "Do the words out of my mouth match the actions my grandkids see in my life?"

INTEGRITY

When words and actions line up well, that's called *integrity*. The character traits of honesty, fairness, truthfulness, sincerity, and trustworthiness will be validated or invalidated by the actions they see. Be careful; they're watching.

During your grandkids' earlier years, they accept anything and everything you say. When they get into their teen years, observation becomes more important. They are beginning to understand that they live in a culture that offers them news, social structures, friends, and media that are all fake. Remember what I mentioned before? Appearance and performance matter more than honesty and honor. Kids don't innately know the difference between counterfeit and real. They learn the difference from trial and error in their earlier adolescent years. This sets them on a course to seek out those relationships that are genuine and authentic.

It is my hope they find someone genuine and authentic in you. Be trustworthy grandparents who can be relied on to be true to their words and deeds.

Here is what I think integrity looks like for grandparents. There is a *vulnerability*, a willingness to suffer hurt, that shows who you really are, coupled with a willingness to express emotion. I used to think the honor given to grandparents came because of their ability to hide their character flaws and escape observation by only visiting for short lengths of time. I thought grandparents smiled, doled out hugs and dollars, and never revealed their true selves. I now think otherwise.

Teens are intrinsically good at sniffing out fakes because they live in a world where you can't (and shouldn't) believe everything you read on the internet or see in a social networking post. They know when they're having the wool pulled over their eyes. Removing yourself from observation isn't the answer. Exposing your true self is. The more they know about who you are, warts and all, the closer the relationship will be. Vulnerability entails being open about who you are. Confessions about struggles and mistakes make you more human. If beloved grandparents failed and still came out okay, then grandchildren can fail and know they'll make it through.

I've met parents and grandparents who never wanted anyone to know they had a previous marriage. Many never let anyone know they had an abortion, smoked pot during college, or got fired from a job. Others hesitate to admit any failure, mistake, blunder, time spent in jail, or illegal activities. Lots of grandparents are cautious to admit past wrongdoing, never realizing that admission and confession clear the path for open and frank relationships. Some are never open about anything, and the mysteries of their lives are taken to their graves. When all faults remain hidden and pushed under the carpet, genuineness and authenticity never happen in a relationship.

Confidence would be another trait of integrity. When grandparents are confident, that confidence can be transferred to their grandchildren. It's about being comfortable in your own skin, and not fearful of someone seeing the real deal. Vulnerability is about being open; confidence is an assuredness of who you are and whose you are.

The trait of *honesty* can be seen when grandparents answer questions or when they ask someone else a question. Honesty means speaking the truth in love, not letting wrongdoings slide, and "telling it like it is" without beating about the bush. Honesty can be seen when a grandmother admits and apologizes for the times she has gossiped or nagged. Honesty can be seen in a grandfather who admits the truth if asked by a grandson if he has ever had a problem with pornography. Honest people return what isn't theirs, answer questions truthfully, and never hide things.

Honest grandparents come clean long before they die. If there's been a *chink in the armor*, it's repaired before they go so their message and legacy remain intact.

Responsibility for one's actions, past and present, is so important in the development of a healthy young adult. Good grandparents make sure they model responsibility, especially because their grandchildren are watching them. Grandparents who model responsibility show their loved ones they never have to worry about cleaning up any messes left behind when grandparents die. There is no unfinished business others have to take care of.

Responsibility means taking the skeletons out of the closet, accepting responsibility for them being there in the first place, and being vulnerable and honest enough to lay claim to what you have done. All this gives you the opportunity to share your story of your redemption.

Another aspect of integrity is a *willingness to take risks*, not be afraid of failure. I'm not talking about financial investments or jumping out of an airplane. I'm talking about taking risks in relationships, confronting what is wrong, speaking the truth in love, exposing your past, risking your reputation for deeper relationship, and taking responsibility for wrongdoing when it may mean some type of consequence.

And lastly, grandparents with integrity *practice what they preach*. Period. They are the opposite of hypocrites and being two-faced. They eliminate falseness and any double standard. They approach life with sincerity. Their words and actions rarely contradict.

How do you rate? Are you a grandfather or grandmother with integrity? Wherever you land on the scale, all the integrity in the world won't impact your grandkids unless you are involved in their lives and give them the opportunity to see you for who you are. Be around. Be steady. Be vulnerable. Be honest. Be responsible. You want your grandchildren to become men and women with integrity. You have to model it first. Your family's legacy largely depends on you.

CONSISTENCY

Integrity takes consistency. You can't be one kind of grandmother in front of the grandkids and another kind of woman when they're not around. Your reputation will precede you. Double standards don't fly.

Here's a personal story. I travel a lot. I'm on and off planes every week speaking somewhere around the country. As a result, I've learned to travel well by myself and am pretty self-sufficient when it comes to planes, trains, and automobiles (and hotels). I can get where I need to go pretty easily and return home without any anxiety or strife because I've learned how to make it all work.

When I travel with others, I'm easily frustrated. They don't travel like I do. They don't want to eat where I want to eat, and they don't follow my time schedule and my way of operating. How rude! Okay, in other words, I'm pretty self-centered when I travel.

I can ruin a vacation before we even get there, yet when I arrive at our destination, I can have a blast and enjoy the time with everyone. I'm not sure they enjoy the time with me because of the way I acted in the process of getting to our destination. It's not where you vacation, but how you get there that counts.

I need to be a man of integrity when I travel solo, and the same man of integrity when I travel with others, especially my family. I have to remind myself that how we get there is more important than the vacation itself in terms of how they perceive me and accept my role in their lives.

Ones who are full of integrity are *secure* enough to speak their mind and stand up for what is right and true. These folks confront wrongdoing and don't tolerate the violation of their core principles. They trust themselves and their belief systems, and don't waste time worrying what others think. They are not swayed but remain steady. They know God is in control, so they don't have to be.

I want my grandkids not to wait to say great things about me after I'm gone to my final destination. I want them to enjoy my presence as we travel together through this thing called life. The more genuine

I am and the more authentic I can be make all the difference. Your grandkids need you to be their model of genuine and authentic. They need you, and they're watching you out of the corners of their eyes.

Chapter 16

WHEN HEALTH GETS IN THE WAY

And surely I am with you always, to the very end of the age.

MATTHEW 28:20 (NIV)

As I wrote this chapter, I was talking with my granddaughter Macie. "You know one day I'm going to kick the bucket, don't you?" I asked.

She said, "Kick the bucket? You mean croak?"

We laughed, but as I looked into her eyes, I saw the reality of that truth. One day, I'm going to be leaving this little girl. I answered her, "Yep, but hopefully not soon!"

"I hope not, Poppa, I hope not," my Macie said.

AS THE YEARS GO BY

When your first grandchild is born, you realize how fast life is moving. You are getting older. A new generation begins, and another eventually ends. Becoming a grandparent is the first signal to us that the aging process will not be passing us by.

I think the second time in life we recognize the passage of time is when we lose a parent. We realize we are slowly creeping to the age where wills, burial plots, retirement, health care, and legacies are more on our minds than ever before.

We also think about our mortality when we begin to have health issues. When a doc looks at you and says, "This is what you have," it's difficult to hear the diagnosis partly because it reminds us one day we will be gone. Sometimes that reminder rattles us more than the actual health issue.

Maybe the hardest marker is the loss of a spouse. After years of being together, the hardest act of love is letting go of the hand of your mate and placing it into the hand of God. The lonely times of loss intensify thoughts that you may be next in line. Grief looms heavy, the price you pay for love. During this time, it is important to take advantage of the precious time left in life to secure your legacy as a grandparent in the hearts of your grandkids.

I have a kidney disease inherited from my mom. She died from it, my grandfather died from it, and my aunt died from it. There's no prevention, and there's no cure. The only hope of not dying from this ailment is a kidney transplant, which just means I will die from some-thing else. No matter what cure is found for whatever disease, there's always another to remind you you're going to die from something. The stark realization that this life on earth will one day end is something no one escapes.

When I first heard I had polycystic kidney disease (PKD), I imme-diately changed my diet, worked out more, changed my lifestyle, and did what I could to prolong my life for as long as possible. I think my main motivation for the lifestyle changes was to make sure I wouldn't leave soon. I don't want to leave soon, even though I know the grim reaper always shows up earlier than expected to your doorstep.

I'm really not afraid of death. At least, I don't think I am. What I am afraid of is how it is going to happen. Chances are, it's not going to happen in an accident. I still wear a seatbelt in the car and a helmet when I ride horses and motorcycles. For me, it will probably be a slow death from a disease where I will have time to prepare how I'll leave by talking about the impending situation, saying good-byes over a period of time, and having all my affairs in order.

Before my mom died, she never wanted to talk about death. I'd visit her in the hospital and at the nursing home, and she would not even broach the subject. I'm not sure if she was scared of death or not willing to accept the fact that she was going to be gone one day. Because she wouldn't accept it, she never had the opportunity to say the things she needed to say to those who loved her. She died within minutes of being told she was going into hospice, probably scared to death (literally) at the thought her time had come.

I think we should look at major health issues another way. Take advantage of them. Put them to good use as reminders that life is short, and the time to leave a legacy is right now! If dementia or Alzheimer's doesn't set in too soon, some health issues give us the opportunity to make amends, call and make things right, and say our final goodbyes.

The inevitability that my life will end motivates and fuels me to want to leave something behind. It pushes me to specifically choose how I spend my precious remaining minutes, and how I speak to and treat those around me. The inevitability of death makes you laugh more, take advantage of conversations, be bolder when you say what needs to be said.

I don't want to be like my mom. I don't want to ignore the inevitable and miss out on the opportunity to share the things deep in my heart, the truths and nuggets of wisdom I learned. My mom's passing didn't motivate me to look at my ancestry and make sure that my affairs were in order; it motivated me to look ahead to the end so I can take advantage of every opportunity before me now. I want my grandkids to remember that I had open and honest conversations about life, from the beginning of our relationship to the end.

Be very careful, then, how you live—not as unwise but as wise, making the most of every opportunity. (EPHESIANS 5:15–16)

I think the wise person, if capable, utilizes every opportunity God allows to leave something behind that can affect the lives of their grandchildren. I don't want to wait until my last day on earth when I'm drooling all over myself or taking my last breath. When I realize it's my grandchildren's last time to hear from their Poppa and my time to wrap it up with the hard goodbyes, I will give assurances they'll be okay and tell them I'll see them soon. I want to usher in hope 'til the very end.

I don't think the last words you say are the most important words of your life, a crescendo, with wisdom just waiting to come forth. I've been around plenty of people who are dying and what they say at the end is not the most significant. My mom's last words to me were, "Mark, your mustache is so white."

That's it? The most important thing she had to say was that? Are you kidding me? The most important words said in a person's life are the ones filled with wisdom and shared over a period of time to children and grandchildren. Most flash-in-the-pan, end-of-life comments will be soon forgotten, but a life well lived will never be disregarded.

I believe the significance of a life can be seen in the words of those who surround the one who is dying, as they reflect on that person's influence.

A MAN NAMED SMITH

I knew a man named Smith Brookhart for more than thirty-five years. When I turned thirty, he turned fifty. All I wanted for my thirtieth birthday was to eat dinner with him. We did. When I turned forty, he turned sixty. Again, all I wanted for my birthday was to eat dinner with him. We did. The same happened when I turned fifty, and I asked for the same when I turned sixty. It happened each decade until I turned sixty. My schedule was crazy, and his health was failing so we only talked by phone. We laughed about the possibility of eating dinner together on my seventieth. We both knew it wasn't going to happen.

A heart transplant extended this dear man's life as far as it could. Diabetes weakened him, walking became difficult, pain racked my friend, and ten years of health issues took their toll. Smith and Gail, his wife of fifty-six years, could see the end of the road. They knew Smith's eternal destination of heaven was not far away. They kept their sons Chip, James, and Tom up to date on every part of their dad's health. The family shared updates and reports with all who asked, including the grandkids that spent most of their life with a Poppa who had health issues.

In spite of his failing health, Smith's responses were encouraging to everyone who knew him. Each morning he would list ten things he was thankful for that day. His welcoming demeanor, his warm hugs, and the way he would say each of his grandkids' names upon their arrival to his home changed their lives. Gail, "GG" to her grandkids, shared how he tenderly loved the grandkids (and really everyone) with jokes and smiles, even in the midst of his battles with health. He loved to laugh and kid around. He made others feel good even when he didn't feel good. Smith and Gail continuously expressed thanks, feeling blessed with what they felt was more than they deserved.

He continued to be a Poppa, to love on his grandkids and influence each of their lives in spite of his major health problems. This strong ol' ox wasn't going to let a failing heart, failing kidneys, and failing body keep him from failing as the Poppa his grandkids knew.

He fulfilled his desire to maintain his role of influence and encouragement in their lives.

Smith was a sharp-witted man, a banker by profession and a bean counter by design. His precise logging of his sugar levels amazed the doctors at the Mayo Clinic. His meticulous scorekeeping of St. Louis Cardinals baseball games impressed all. He expressed his reasoned responses with authority, his opinions with discernment (most of the time), his faith with conviction, and his compassion with thoughtfulness. His sons knew this well. His grandkids saw him as a hero, almost larger than life itself.

In spite of his frailties, he witnessed to others about the Lord, and a couple dozen folks commented how they strengthened their walk with God as a result of seeing Smith wander through this maze of health challenges.

Smith knew that time on earth is short. The last ten days of Smith's life were spent in a hospital. When his kidneys started to fail, the family members called, Skyped, and flocked to his bedside to say goodbye to their Poppa. He had been upfront and honest about his condition, and he shared the reality of his dying as much as he shared about living. This brave man imparted to his grandkids many things they will never forget.

He understood that upon receiving a new heart, he was living in *overtime*, in extended play. That's when he dedicated his remaining days to being part of his grandkids' lives. He spent time talking about everything that was happening with him. At the very end, it was not his last words that meant the most, but all he gave throughout his life. Smith lived and died well. He knew the memories he etched on the hearts of his grandkids would have to suffice once the life he shared with them was over.

His grandson Stewart said, "What God did with Poppa was the same thing that Michelangelo did with a frayed, imperfect piece of stone. He took it and created the beautiful masterpiece, *David*."

A few months after his Poppa died, young grandson Everett said, "You know, I really miss Poppa. I love coming here, but it's not the same. Can we get a substitute?"

An older granddaughter Casey shared, "He was incredible. Every time I walked into a room, Poppa welcomed me with a loving smile and voice, saying, 'How's my Casey Ann?' That would make me feel special. He was very intentional about conversations, very interested in what we were learning."

Grandson Parker said, "He didn't make a big deal out of his health stuff, so most of our discussions were just normal. Whenever I think of Poppa, I think of tough love. I think of Poppa all the time."

Granddaughter Allison stated, "When I had my last conversation with him, I let him know that I was fearful of him leaving and not being at my college graduation, or meeting his great-grandkids, or being at my wedding. His response was that life on earth was fleeting, just a vapor, and soon we will all be together again. He told me he was grateful to be a part of my life and assured me that I was going to be okay. I was never more proud to be his granddaughter."

High school graduate Smith IV shared, "The thing that I remember the most is how Poppa loved me, cared for me, and listened to all that I had to say."

When eleven-year-old grandson Anderson got on the phone to tell his Poppa goodbye for the last time, he said he needed to be brave, just like Poppa showed him.

The common thread that ran through each of these grandkids' comments was how Smith, their beloved Poppa, made them all feel special, a theme each grandchild felt and knew in his or her heart.

WHEN POOR HEALTH FINALLY WINS THE BATTLE...ON THIS SIDE

The death of a grandparent is often a grandchild's first experience of watching the end of the cycle of life. That's why the experience has such an impact on kids. Watching a grandparent with health issues is real life. It can be seen, understood, and felt. Having a grandparent die feels surreal, a new experience that transitions a child from concrete to abstract thinking. Death is foreign, unusual, strange, and surreal because it is not a common experience for them.

An important aspect of managing health issues with grandkids is helping them understand. Have those comments and discussions that prepare them for life to end one day. When you get sick and have health issues, don't hesitate to help a grandchild come to an understanding of what's happening with you.

Toward the end of your life, it's also important to give them assurance. Assurance that all is going to be okay, that you're going to be fine in the arms of Jesus. Help them see that, as you have trusted Christ with your life, they are going to have to trust Him as well when you leave them. Help your grandchild feel like hope is not lost, but your passing will be hope fulfilled.

Health issues (sigh). Two of Smith's grandkids ended seeing their grandfather with this, and it's how I hope we are all described by our grandchildren long after we are gone. *Poppa fought like a warrior to be with us so we would all get to know him.*

And fight my friend Smith did. He fought to influence his grandkids to walk in a manner that is worthy of God, and to love family like there's no tomorrow.

What are you doing to leave that same kind of legacy?

PART IV

GRANDPARENTS: DON'T SAVE WHAT IS THE BEST FOR LAST

Chapter 17

DON'T SAVE THE BEST FOR LAST

For where your treasure is, there your heart will be also.

LUKE 12:34 (KJV)

During the last ten years of my mom's life, she always told me how fast time flies and how it flies even faster with each passing day. Now that I'm in my sixties, I can comprehend what she was trying to tell me. Why, it seems like I'm filling thirty-day prescriptions every other day. Sixty seconds seem like thirty. It feels like Christmas is every other month, and my teeth are getting cleaned every other week. Life is sure speeding up.

Before you know it, that ol' body of yours will begin to wither, age will remind you of your limitations, and you'll be a number you never thought possible, wondering *where did all the time go?* The relentless marching on of the aging process will come at you through medical issues, gray hair, wrinkles, failing eyesight, droopy skin, and loss of hearing. Embracing the frailty of life and the promise of it one day ending can change who you are, how you are perceived, and the impact you will have on others.

Everything you own will one day be given away. All your accumulations, money, collections, clothes, memorabilia—all of it—will be given away to family and friends, if not sold to complete strangers. Comforting thought, isn't it?

After my mom died, we moved my dad into a retirement village. He was realizing that, as he put it, "The house is pretty quiet." And we could tell it was taking a toll on him. As we moved him and all the belongings gathered throughout 62 years of marriage, Dad stated that he no longer needed much. Just his computer, a couple pieces of furniture, and a pot to cook in. Perhaps the loss of a spouse makes you realize how frivolous things are. He reeled from his own grief and the prospect of now living life on his own in a strange new place.

My siblings and I talked about what we each wanted from my parents' lifelong collection of belongings. Surprisingly, we didn't want much. Still, the thought of just giving it all away or selling it to others felt tough to process. We, too, were grieving the loss.

I rented a trailer and brought home all the furniture and belongings to Texas, where a few months later we had a garage sale and gave away much of my mom's history to people she never knew or met. Then it hit me: the collection of all the stuff in our lives is just that—*stuff*.

I asked my kids what they wanted of mine when I die. My daughter couldn't think of anything. My son told me he wanted my guns and a few pairs of my boots. I remember saying, "That's it? That's all you want? Just those things?"

He answered, "Yep, that's about it."

In 1974, I lost all my belongings to a tornado in Tulsa, Oklahoma. That event taught me about the value of things. My son's comments about what he wanted from my belongings showed me what holds true value. It isn't what I've been collecting all my life.

The most valuable possessions in life aren't things, aren't just stuff. They're relationships. The pursuit of relationships is fundamental to God's plan for us all and what he values most.

GIVE IT ALL AWAY

So here's my first piece of advice in this chapter: Give it away. Give your time, your resources, and your efforts to those around you. In particular, give to your grandkids while they have the time to appreciate it and you have your health to enjoy the giving.

Now, I'm one who believes in taking care of yourself financially. I'm a finance guy from the University of Tulsa who embraces what John Wesley stated a couple of centuries ago, that one should, "Earn all you can, save all you can, give all you can."

I'm a believer in financial security, especially as one enters retirement. But I'm all about sharing as well, and there is nothing more rewarding or which carries a greater impact than sharing with your family.

Here's a proverb for all you grandparents.

A good person leaves an inheritance for their children's children.
(PROVERBS 13:22)

I'm convinced of this. And I'm convinced this verse isn't just talking about leaving money, if it's talking about that at all. It's about leaving a legacy, an heirloom, a tradition, and a heritage, something that lasts in the souls of your grandkids.

Many times I wondered what it would have been like to have a heart full of memories of experiences with my parents and grandparents. I've speculated at what I could have done earlier in my life if someone had given me five thousand dollars when I got married and how that would have helped in so many ways. I've pondered what it would have been like to have grandparents give me something that was dear to them; something passed on that meant something to them. I've wondered what messages I would have gotten if a grandparent had given me advice, taken the time to help in some fashion, or shown me an example of what it was like to value relationships and how to give.

My grandkids challenge me to think about whether I am doing those very things today. The times I wondered what I would have received have now been transformed into thinking about whether I am giving and changing my grandchildren's world with my time, resources, and efforts. That's how a grandparent leaves a legacy.

DON'T WAIT TO GIVE IT AWAY

Here's my second piece of advice for this chapter: Don't wait. Don't save the best for last. You might just miss it.

David Muth and I met when his daughter came to live with us at Heartlight ten years ago. We hit it off the moment we met. His winsome personality was a joy to be around, and you could see his love for his family. There was always a spark of humor amid his wisdom-filled conversations. We laughed. We laughed a lot together.

David knew I love wine and we shared bottles of specialty wines throughout the years whenever we got together. We sent wine to each other on holidays or birthdays. Sitting on my back porch, surely, we figured out the deep, hidden issues of life, God, and the souls of men over glasses of fine wine. We had the kind of deep discussions I don't have with many.

David collected wine and always told me about the bottles he was saving for a special occasion. I'm sure I added a few to his *special occasion* collection, all neatly and precisely tucked away in his wine refrigerator for exclusive times of honor and celebration.

He and his wife, Amy, served on our board of directors at Heartlight, which sometimes felt like an excuse to get together and catch up on our very different lives. His life was the busy life of a hospital anesthesiologist. Mine was the founder of a ranch for struggling teens.

David called me one afternoon to share that he had just been diagnosed with Parkinson's disease. As he described it, this was the Parkinson's that wasn't the *shaky* kind, but one that, over time, would deteriorate the organs in his body. He said that most people with his diagnosis didn't live more than five or six years. He was going to have to retire at fifty-two and planned to move to Anna Maria Island, Florida, where he would face the challenges of his remaining years with Parkinson's.

After a couple of years of keeping up over the phone, and getting updates on his condition, I decided I needed to spend some time with him at his home in Florida. I committed to doing so every couple of months. I'd travel to see him at the tail end of speaking engagements or make a stopover in Tampa on the way back home.

The first time I got there to see him and Amy, I took him an expensive bottle of wine (Opus) to be used for a special occasion. He tucked it away in his wine cache. At that point in his Parkinson's journey, we always pulled out bottles not designated for special occasions and enjoyed them over the same deep discussions. We also watched movies and laughed until our bellies hurt.

Over time, Parkinson's took Dave down further and further. On one of my trips to see him, he said, "Let's take out one of those bottles I've been saving for a special occasion and have that tonight." He let me know that he had a 1960 Port, a bottle that was fifty-five years old and was his Cadillac of wines. He'd had it most of his adult life and kept it for just the right time to drink it. And now I'd be the one to share that moment with him.

His hands had gotten to where he couldn't open the bottle, and he asked me to do the honors. As I opened the bottle and began to pour the wine, we were both quick to notice the wine had gone bad. Basically, it had turned to mush. The look of disappointment on his face is one I will never forget. All the hope he held onto for so many years of enjoying that special bottle of wine was dashed.

Next, he said, "Well, I have a 1968 Bordeaux [French] I've been saving."

I opened it up and much to our surprise, it had gone bad as well.

He continued, "Well, I have a 1974 Barolo I've been saving for a special occasion. Let's open up that one." We did, and much to our shock, it had gone bad as well.

"Well, I have a 1992 Screaming Eagle from Napa I've been saving for a special occasion. Let's give that one a shot." We did, and to our dismay, the same thing happened. David began to realize that what he had been saving for was all in vain.

After a couple more bottles of wine brought the same ending, I asked David if we could just open the bottle I had brought him months ago—that Opus I gave him for a special occasion. He relented, and we both enjoyed.

That night as I lay awake in David and Amy's guest bedroom, I kept thinking over and over about what lesson was to be learned from what just happened. This is what I concluded: Don't save for that *special occasion* because the *special occasion* is today.

The fact that we were both together that day was occasion enough to enjoy the very best. I committed to this. Anytime someone comes to my home and we share wine, I'm going to pull out the very best and most expensive bottle of wine I have and serve it. I'm not going to wait for any *special occasion* because that *special occasion* is now. This moment.

Don't wait until you're no longer busy; that will never happen.

Don't wait until that special occasion; it is happening around you every day.

Don't wait until you can find the time; it passes way too quickly.

Don't miss the opportunity during your grandkids' teen years; it will be gone too soon.

You will never be appreciated more, or have a greater impact on, the ones you are with today.

Chapter 18

GIVING THE BIG-PICTURE PERSPECTIVE TO THEIR TEENAGER WORLD

The beginning of wisdom is this: Get wisdom.

Though it cost all you have, get understanding.

PROVERBS 4:7 (NIV)

Taylor Swift is one of the bestselling country/pop artists of all time. She is the recipient of ten Grammy Awards, twenty-one Billboard Music Awards, eleven Country Music Association Awards, and too many other awards to list. My two granddaughters could care less about awards. They were just dying to see this popular artist perform. When they found out T-Swizzle was coming to an arena just a few miles from where we all lived, no one would rest until we bought tickets.

My daughter was charged with purchasing the tickets, which she quickly did just before the concert sold out. The day came, and the five of us set off for the concert: two little girls dressed like Taylor, one mom wanting to please her kids, and two grandparents who love country music and wanted to see Taylor Swift.

Jan and I have been to quite a few concerts throughout our lives, and the challenge of each ticket purchase is to get as close to the front of the venue as possible or at least reasonably close enough to recognize the performer as something more than just a dot on the stage. Ever since our first date to a Led Zeppelin concert in 1971, Jan has always asked, "Did you get good seats?" Of course, I would glow with pride when sharing how close we would be to the artists and how great our seats would be. I love the front-row view at any concert.

My daughter didn't have this in mind when she purchased the tickets for the Taylor Swift concert. When we entered the 14,000-seat arena, we trudged up and up to our seats, farther and farther from the stage, finally ending up in the top section in the very last row of seats. I mean, the back of my head was touching concrete. You couldn't get any farther back. There I sat, the only man in the whole arena, in the worst seats in the house. The stage appeared to be over a mile away.

I looked at my daughter with a *What-are-these-seats?* kind of look and she looked back at me with *These-are-the-only-seats-I-could purchase* look. Then came the now famous and unforgettable statement. Macie, my five-year-old granddaughter looked around and said with wonder, "Poppa, these are the best seats in the whole place. You can see everything from here!"

IT'S ALL ABOUT PERSPECTIVE

Perspective. It was all in the perspective—that big-picture view that helps you see more than what is evident, and beyond that which is right before you.

For teens today, perspective has been lost. The impact of today's actions on one's later life are largely ignored because parents have lost their ability to influence their kids through giving them a *bigger picture* perspective in their parenting relationship.

Moms and dads have moved from parenting to *peer-enting* in an attempt to try to create good relationships that weren't there when they were raised. This movement, coupled with a teen's perception of not needing to respect and support those in authority, has now cut the legs off moms' and dads' abilities to guide and influence. Teens now rely more on their peers than they do their parents, creating a *blind leading the blind* scenario that hardly fosters maturity, does not encourage responsibility, and doesn't form a great fountain of wisdom.

Psychologist and family physician Leonard Sax states in his wonderful and insightful book, *The Collapse of Parenting*:

> The most serious consequence of the shift from a parenting-oriented culture to a peer-oriented culture is that parents no longer are able to provide that big picture to their children.[9]

See where I'm headed?

I'm not saying parents are ineffective in their parenting. I am on the road for 200 speaking events every year. At these events, I try to help moms and dads better understand the teen world, and help them understand why this culture is trying to undermine them as parents.

I believe that parents have to be relational in their approach to their teens. They can't lead in such an authoritarian way that it pushes their child away. Instead, they need to use their God-given authority in a relational way to lead and empower their teens to be respecters of the whole family structure. And they need backup. Backup that supports and encourages understanding.

Parents have their hands and plates full. What their teens don't need is another set of parents to complicate the problems caused by a culture trying to flip their roles. What teens and parents need are people who can help bring perspective and wisdom into the family situation and assist parents by helping their kids and *your* grandkids find purpose and meaning in their lives. The difference between parental and grandparental wisdom is that an older perspective brings a generation of mistakes, learning, and on-the-job education to the mix. And experienced grandparents can help their kids not make the same mistakes they did.

The people they need are you, their loving grandparents.

ALL THEY NEED IS YOU…BUT WITHOUT THE CRITICISM

I bet you've stated sometime in the last few years how glad you are that you don't have to grow up in this adolescent culture. I know I would have been a mess in my junior high school years if I had access to some of the imagery and information that our grandkids are exposed to on a daily basis.

Well, your grandkids have to grow up in this culture. They have to function and survive in a world that is different from the world their parents and grandparents grew up in. That doesn't mean it is worse or bad or doomed. It just means it's different.

Different means you must approach your grandkids from another angle, one that allows you to be invited to speak truth into their lives. Not only must you develop an understanding of what is happening in their culture, but you also have to possess the ability to see beyond what is right in front of them and offer a voice of wisdom that will guide and direct your grandkids.

- That maybe the world isn't nearly as bad as they think it is.
- That the problems before them aren't as big as they feel they are.
- That just because they're hurting, doesn't mean their life is over.
- That challenges before them might really be new opportunities for them to embrace.

You can give them *big picture* perspective. They may have the internet—but you have experience. They may be able to ask Siri or Alexa, but no tech gadget can speak truths about the meaning of life, love, and relationships. You can.

The world they live in is quite different from the one we grew up in. But it's all they know. What is totally foreign to you is absolutely common to them. Gaining an understanding of their world and their culture helps in your approach to drawing them to you as a source of wisdom.

Let me share a few of the challenges our teens face today. Not only is there a lack of respect for authority, but there is also an extreme lack of respect for one another. Media depicts politicians, pastors, police officers, teachers, administrators, businessmen and -women, coaches, priests, and parents as people not worthy of respect. Our Western culture encourages voicing disrespect of anything and anyone you don't agree with. Political correctness hampers the ability to speak freely, and the *rights of all* have so far encouraged more division than unity.

The difficulty with this culture of disrespect is that the wise people in authority have already been eliminated from a teen's circle of influence before any of that wisdom can be transferred.

The amount of information at everyone's fingertips has overloaded our lives. Consider the number of sources of information you had when you were growing up—three main TV stations, a newspaper, and the radio. Now there are countless ways to find out everything about anything you want. The need to get information from friends and family is almost nil. Teens today are stuffed with information yet starving for wisdom.

Think about it. Communication is at our fingertips twenty-four hours a day, seven days a week. Text messaging, apps, social media, and image messaging sites are changing the way people communicate. Relationships that are started on dating sites now make up over fifty percent of the marriages in the U.S. Millions of pictures are sent on a daily basis, millions of videos posted on anything you can think of. Social networking sites are changing the social structure of the adolescent world, providing a false sense of connection with one another. Pornography and sexually explicit videos are readily available, changing the rules of modesty and permissible sexual behavior.

Teens live in a culture where alternative lifestyles are promoted and prevalent. Gender confusion abounds. Young men hardly know what it means to be a man, and young girls struggle to know what it is to be a woman.

Role models almost don't exist. Teens are becoming more and more frail. Everyone wants to be famous. Adolescents are moving more and more toward being overweight, out of shape, and suicidal. More kids take medication than ever before.

You can spend time with your teen grandkids arguing any one of the preceding points, sharing everything that is wrong with this teen culture, but that won't build the relationship. Even though it's all true, you will accomplish nothing except to send a clear message that you are disconnected, a *fuddy-duddy*, an old-timer lost in a new generation, or one who is just clueless. Yes, you can spend all your time criticizing their culture, but it will get you nowhere.

PET PEEVES

Do you have pet peeves? I have pet peeves. There are some things that just bug me and seem odd to me. I know it's a part of getting older, but there are just some elements of this culture that scream, "Will someone just pay attention to me!" I know it's a result of this performance-driven and appearance-focused world our grandkids live in.

Here's what bugs me: It feels as if people are trying to outdo and outshine one another on the internet, seeking the false approval of social media followers instead of building real relationships with loved ones right in front of them. There are individual posts on internet social networking sites that scream, "Will someone just look at me? Will someone just value me?"

I see grandkids going to proms who have very little desire about wanting to dress up and show up. I see pictures and videos of couples' wedding showers that just seem odd to me. It seems like every pregnancy now automatically comes with a *gender reveal* party. And don't get me started on the videos of people getting engaged that sometime seem more about putting on an over-the-top show than about recording a special moment of their love for each other.

Am I revealing my age a bit? I'm sure you can list some things that bug you as well. Your pet peeves may differ from my list, but I think we all have things that bother us. Here's the best way I can handle those cultural differences and things I don't always agree with—I can keep my mouth shut. Why on earth would I do that? Why would I let my grandkids and this culture get away with all this *nonsense* when I know better? Because the Bible tells me so.

*Even fools are thought wise when they keep silent; with their mouths shut, they seem intelligent. (*PROVERBS *17:28, NLT)*

Yep, sometimes we communicate loudest and smartest when we say nothing at all. Your role as a grandparent isn't to point out everything that's wrong with this country, this culture, and the way the world is going. Your role is to show, not lecture, your grandkids about a different perspective on a world that may look crazy to us but to them appears normal.

YOUR APPROACH IN A "CRAZY TO YOU" BUT "SANE TO THEM" WORLD

Instead of criticizing and comparing and complaining about the world your teen grandchildren are growing up in, spend time gaining an understanding of the culture's impact on them. That understanding gives you the chance to offer the same moral and spiritual truths as their parents, but from a different angle that will help solidify the transfer of biblical truths, moral principles, and godly wisdom that carry on the legacy of your family.

Teens live in a world searching for someone, anyone, to listen and watch. They long for someone who understands the world and will help them understand it. They need someone who looks at life from a bigger-picture perspective and compassionately communicates the path to take to avoid mistakes and choices that can affect their lives negatively.

Perspective.

Oh yeah, back to that Taylor Swift concert. We were sitting in the back, right? My head was banging against the concrete as 13,997 little girls around me screamed at the top of their lungs throughout the whole show. Remember, these were the worst seats in the house (from my perspective). My little Macie, bless her heart, thought they were the best.

Forty-five minutes into the concert, my perspective changed too. Much to our surprise, Taylor Swift suddenly stood singing ten feet away from us. She had come to the back (the very back) of the venue to sing right to everyone seated a million miles away from the stage. (I now see why so many adore this young lady; she loves her fans.)

Macie looked at me, eyes shining, and said, "See, Poppa, I told you these were the best seats!" She was right.

They were the best seats in the house.

It was all in the perspective.

Chapter 19

WHAT IS YOUR AGENDA?

Spend time with the wise and you will become wise,

but the friends of fools will suffer.

Proverbs 13:20 (NCV)

People have a propensity to complain about the youth of *today*. They always have. Throughout history, one can easily find moaning and groaning about these *young people* and how their attitudes and actions are destroying the very moral fiber of our country. We, meaning any of us who are older than teenagers and millennials, tend to recall our time of adolescence as a wonderful time of innocence and wonder. Nothing we did was *that bad*, certainly not as damaging and destructive as the practices of youth today. We adopt an all-is-lost attitude, thinking we are living in the worst times there have ever been.

When I think back to the time I grew up in New Orleans in the 1960s, I vividly remember The Beatles (I saw them in City Park on September 16, 1964), the Beach Boys, the first man to walk on the moon, *The Ed Sullivan Show*, *Mary Poppins*, *The Beverly Hillbillies*, Walt Disney, Debbie Meyer swimming in the 1968 Olympics in Mexico City, Woodstock, James Bond movies, and *The Dirty Dozen*, just to name a few memories. Those are what instantly come to my mind.

When I reflect more deeply, I remember what else went on during the '60s. I come to the somewhat different conclusion that perhaps those good ol' days probably weren't as good as I thought. Vietnam, the assassination of President John F. Kennedy, the later assassination of his brother Senator Bobby Kennedy, the assassination of Martin Luther King Jr, Louisiana's Hurricane Camille, the Bay of Pigs invasion, the Manson murders, and riots in Chicago and Detroit. Not the good ol' days, but days and years when an entire nation experienced a huge cultural shift.

COMPLAINING ABOUT THE BAD NEW DAYS

Maybe it wasn't so good back then. Maybe, just maybe, it's not so bad now. Times are different. Very different. But different doesn't warrant instant judgment. Positive change rarely comes out of negative criticism. In other words, complaining doesn't fix anything.

Complaining about the youth of today is nothing new. This is what Peter the Hermit said in a sermon he preached during his lifetime. (No, Peter the Hermit was not one of Herman's Hermits.)

"The world is passing through troublous times. The young people of today think of nothing but themselves. They have no reverence for parents or old age. They are impatient of all restraint. They talk as if they knew everything, and what passes for wisdom with us is foolishness with them. As for the girls, they are forward, immodest and unladylike in speech, behavior, and dress."[10]

French priest Peter the Hermit played a key role during the First Crusade and delivered this sermon (and his perspective on youth) more than five hundred years ago!

If you're like me, you don't want to complain all the time about the culture of teens today. Who wants to be seen as the crotchety, decrepit Grandpa instead of the fun, cool one? Instead, I want to understand today's youth culture, not frame it as an evil culture with no hope. If I see it like that, not only am I judging my grandkids and their friends, but also, what hope will they have for their own futures?

I want to understand so I can help my grandkids navigate through today's times that seem so different from the world I grew up in yet are so similar in their challenges. One of the major challenges remains to bring timeless truth and wisdom to an ever-changing world of influence. This challenge is not the sole goal of grandparenting. First and foremost, the intent is to connect with your grandchildren during their teen years. You can be the connection that offers hope.

RELATIONSHIP BUILDING ISN'T LIKE FALLING OFF A LOG

You can complain about the youth of today. However, complaining always blocks the connection. Instead, I suggest you pursue ways of connecting that will move your grandchildren to bond with you so strongly that you will be able to offer them what they cannot get from any other person in the world.

I've found connection doesn't automatically happen because you are a grandparent or parent. Deep engagement isn't inherited; it's cultivated. You cultivate it every time you are intentional in reaching out to your grandchildren in ways that make them want to reach back. When you are intentional about asking for an invitation into their world instead of trying to drag them out of it and into yours, you can help your grandchildren get to the places they want to be. You can also help keep them from ending up in places they don't want to be.

This process begins with grandparents asking questions. Hopefully, it then blossoms into a relationship where the grandchild asks the questions. This exchange is a process, one I've learned from my relationships with thousands of teens.

There are five necessary steps in this connecting with your adolescent (and sometimes older) grandkids. Let's unpack them a little here.

Show Interest Instead of Setting Up Your Agenda

During the first years of our grandkids' lives, I think we get involved for our own selfish reasons. We love their cuteness, enjoy watching them grow, and feel ecstatic when they give us a name, no matter how corny or funny those names may be. (I know one set of grandparents whose grandson thought *Grandma* and *Grandpa* sounded like *Gravy* and *Meatball*. The names stuck.) Grandbabies make us feel good, look good, and put smiles on our faces. I don't think there's anything wrong with our intentions at this point. It's pretty normal to be proud of your offspring.

Then those cute little grandkids turn twelve, and it all begins to change. That is exactly when we grandparents better change right with them. Adolescence is a critical point that could determine your level of involvement in the rest of their lives. During this critical time, you have to shift the focus of your relationship from your interests to theirs.

If your grandchild feels for a moment that your purpose and intent in their life are just to transfer all the wisdom you've gained in life, you will bore them to tears. You will quickly find yourself irrelevant in their lives. It will be apparent to them that you are in this thing to fulfill your own agenda, not because you care about them. They will see it as nothing more than another program that is more about you than them. They can smell that a mile away. You may think adolescents and teens have no common sense, but they can be incredibly savvy. And they can know genuineness when they see it. Remember, grandparenting is not about you. It's about your grandkids.

Remember the question is always, What is *your* agenda? It interprets the rest of this book's chapter.

Paul writes about this when he says to the Philippians,

> *Do nothing out of selfish ambition or vain conceit. Rather, in humility value others above yourselves, not looking to your own interests but each of you to the interests of the others.* (PHILIPPIANS 2:3–4)

After *shifting* your focus to them, you need to *shift* the focus of your interest. One of the hardest challenges of grandparenting is sharing the wisdom you have gathered through life in a way that applies to *their* world and *their* culture, not the world you grew up in and learned from.

I know teens show an interest in me because I have an interest in them. They are longing for someone to listen to their hearts and their stories. They want to be loved and cared for in ways other than those in Gary Chapman's *Five Love Languages*. They want to do things together. They want to eat where they want to eat, go where they want to go, and have someone help them fulfill their dreams. Showing interest in your grandkids isn't something you do; it must become who you are.

Adapt to Their World

Okay, so you live in a world of immodest girls who are unladylike in their behavior, foolish boys who think only of themselves, a world where kids have a great sense of entitlement. They are impatient, know everything, and hardly respect their elders. That's exactly how Peter the Hermit (mentioned previously) saw way back around A.D. 1080. That is the world of kids today, and in every age, it seems. It was in yours. The difference for you now is that your grandkids have to live in it.

When I say adapt, I'm not telling you to scrap your standards or beliefs and discard what you hold to be true and valuable. I am telling you that your message can't be outdated, out of touch, and from outer space in regard to their world. You can't be a stick (in the mud), but you must be pliable and adjustable to wrap around the issues they are facing. This isn't a time for criticism. It's an opportunity to speak into their life without judging who they are because they think differently from you.

You'll be like the major department stores and companies we see going belly up. They couldn't adapt to the changing times to keep up with the transformation and conversion of a culture that has made some pretty extreme shifts in the last few years. So they closed up shop. Don't close the doors on the teens you love.

If your message is relevant, don't change your content. Do change the way you approach it and say it so the intended recipients of the message can embrace the message, engage with applicability, and value the effectiveness of the wisdom shared.

As I travel across North America, I see a great decline in church attendance by those about to graduate from high school and those in their late teens. There are about a million kids in the seventh-grade youth program and about four who remain in the church by their senior year. Okay, I may be exaggerating and joking a little here, but there is a major drop. This age group tends to take a hiatus from church, and I think they do so for a couple of adaptability reasons.

The first reason churches don't adapt is that many teens believe the church isn't that important. The busyness of their schedules coupled with other interests crowd out time for church and church-related activities. The second reason is that youth leaders have been slow to adapt the gospel message to an age group that has gone through major and radical ways that teens socialize and communicate.

- Teens don't care about dating as much as they used to.
- Bullying has become a way of life for many.

- Connections happen more and more through networking sites than personal interactions.
- Peer communication is more through posts and texts than the phone functions of cells.
- The bombardment of information is overwhelming and blurs what is true and what is not.
- New ways of entertainment fill time once spent in personal socialization.
- Everyone has new ways to spew their criticism or share their opinion.

I'm not faulting youth leaders. Most are committed people dedicated to ministry to the young people of today. But this intense and overwhelming cultural shift has caught them off guard. This tsunami wave of negative influence has come ashore and flooded the teen culture and changed the landscape of adolescence. And youth leaders are having a tough time keeping up with the rate of changes.

- The definition of modesty has changed.
- Pornography, with 4.3 million porn sites, is changing the perceptions of adolescence.
- Gender issues are confusing the message of marriage for many teens.
- Legalization of marijuana is giving permission for what once was illegal.
- The exposure to more and more various lifestyles challenges a grandparent's (and teen's) value system.

But these two reasons speak volumes to the need for the adaptability of the message to a new, tech-savvy but relationship-poor generation that are often overwhelmed by life as they know it.

Adaptability is more than the pastor wearing an untucked shirt and ripped or even skinny jeans. It's more than current and contemporary worship songs with lights down low and a few candles burning through the fog machine. It is understanding the needs and speaking directly to the issues that teens are facing, then giving directives that speak to those problems that matter to teens.

Build Relationships

You'll hear me repeat the word *relationship* a lot in this book. A real relationship takes the investment of time, effort, and resources as mentioned earlier in this book. The key word is *investment*. The focus of that investment has to be the benefit of the grandchild, motivated out of love for that child.

Paul wrote to the Thessalonians and said,

> *"We loved you so much that we shared with you not only God's Good News but our own lives, too."* (1 Thessalonians 2:8 NLT)

Teens are looking for deeper relationships. They long for genuineness and authenticity in relationships with older adults who are comfortable in their own skin. For relationships that offer something more than only correction when they make mistakes or blunders in their decision-making. They desire someone who is frank enough to share an honest opinion and courageous to speak the truth in love when issues arise because they know the motivation comes from a deep empathy for their plight.

If you have a discipline problem, you have a relationship problem. If you have a respect problem, you have a relationship problem. If you have an obedience problem, you have a relationship problem. In a relationship, you will see the problems, and in a relationship, you will discover a teen's motivation for change. A teen does not change because of an authoritarian approach. A teen listens to authority because of relationship.

Your relationship with your grandchildren could be the only voice of wisdom they listen to during a time of their lives when they aren't listening to God or any other member of their family. You could be the only attachment they have to the family when they feel distant from siblings and parents who are disappointed and upset with their choices.

The need to have fun together is paramount. How much you laugh together is a good measurement of your relationship. The amount of communication between you and your grandchildren will be an indicator of how healthy your relationship is.

So learn every way possible to communicate as a grandparent, not as a parent. Your role is not to be a second set of parents, but one who encourages and communicates hope and perspective. As you move into your later years, be sure to try to keep up with technology so you maintain and entertain new forms of communication. If you don't know how to do this, ask the kids. They'll be happy to teach you, and it will give you an opportunity to learn something new together.

Create Connection

The connection I'm talking about is the next step in the relationship with your grandchild. This connection is more than you making things happen. It's when communication, effort, and desire to spend time together become a two-way street. This is what you want to happen with your teenage grandchildren. It is more important than the message you have to share. It has to be cultivated . . . and watered . . . and fertilized . . . and allowed to grow.

Let me give you an example. My granddaughter Maile knows the lyrics to every current country song. How she does it, I'll never know. Because of her love for this genre of music, I joined the Country Music Association so we could attend the Country Music Awards every year. I purchase the tickets, book the flight, and we go. We laugh, take pictures, laugh more, cheer on the artists, and leave Nashville with memories that will last her a lifetime. I purchase shirts and programs for her and provide opportunities for her to meet as many artists as I can. It's all for one purpose—to keep the connection we've found and hopefully nurture it until my dying day.

We text each other with news about upcoming concerts and up-and-coming artists. We look together for the next opportunity to spend time at these events. The result? A special connection that ties our hearts together. It is a tie that binds when other things in her life aren't quite as she or her parents hope they will be. The connection has been a lifeline for Maile and me.

So here are some things I've learned about connection with grandkids:

- Connection is more than just a relationship; it's a pipeline for providing hope and direction.
- Connection is not measured by the number of pictures of your grandchild you post on your social networking sites.
- Connection is not just appearing to have a relationship; connection is having the relationship that is effortless in its pursuit and involvement with one another.
- Connection is not an opportunity for correction; it's a platform for guidance.
- Connection is a mutual love for one another established because a grandparent determines to pour life and love into a teen who longs to be a participating member of a family.

Invite Questions

When I initially show interest in any teen, including my grandkids, I do it by asking questions about his or her life, thoughts, and heart. You know the art of questioning is important to me the way I've talked about it in this book. It's not the interrogating type of questioning that puts kids on the spot or makes them feel like I'm looking for problems, but the type of questions that convey value.

The questions I ask also give them an example of what's it like to show interest in others, to consider others more important than oneself.

My hope is they'll begin to ask me questions because they see me as a grandparent full of wisdom (not correction), one who genuinely is focused on bettering their lives, one who is willing to put his money where his mouth is to share time, effort, and resources to further the relationship.

This is what I want to happen: I want them to start asking me questions. You'll know you have a connection when your grandkids start asking in some shape or form any of the following questions:
- "Can you keep a secret?"
- "Can I tell you something?"
- "Hey, want to get together for dinner?"
- "Grandpa, did you ever smoke pot or get drunk?"
- "Grandma, did you and Grandpa ever have sex before you got married?"
- "Grandpa, what if I marry the wrong person?"
- "Grandma, did you ever fall away from Jesus . . . I mean, just not get it sometimes?"
- "Hey, what's the one life lesson you've found to be the most important?"

As a grandparent, this is what you've been waiting for. It's their invitation to you to speak the truth (however painful that may be) into their lives. They're asking because they want answers. Their questions will let you know there is a connection, and they want wisdom.

BE A PLACE OF SAFETY

Your genuineness and authenticity will create a "safe harbor" where your teen grandchildren can come to know you and feel more open to share about the issues in their lives. It is at that time that you'll be able to share the wisdom you possess and the life skills that you have developed through the years.

They are learning. You can be a safe place, a sounding board as they learn how to function in their culture in a healthy way. They're just doing it differently than you did. I assure you they will learn what they need to learn to survive in their world. Hopefully they'll do it with a foundation of wisdom that you share with them, so their learning isn't quite as painful as your acquisition of wisdom was. It's one of the greatest challenges of grandparents, but so well worth the effort.

Quit complaining about your grandkids. Begin the trek to building a relationship that connects you to the very heart of your grandchildren. Remember, it's not about what you *do*, and it's not necessarily about what you *say*. It's more about who you *are* in the presence of your grandkids.

Chapter 20

A PLACE OF RETREAT CAN BE A HAVEN

Come to me, all you who are weary and burdened, and I

will give you rest. Take my yoke upon you and learn from me,

for I am gentle and humble in heart, and you will find rest for

your souls. For my yoke is easy and my burden is light.

MATTHEW 11:28–30 (NIV)

Recently I sat in a living room with a crowd of people who had come to see two older folks, grandparents who had gotten up there in years (each in their nineties). Four teens were in the room and some fifty-something siblings. Everyone listened as these two oldsters told all their medical stories of the previous six months. We all heard about hemorrhoids, calluses, bunions, bum knees, poor eyesight, hearing loss, something getting burned off, urine samples, and the need for another colonoscopy, endoscopy, and polyps removal. Getting old is not for the faint of heart.

I sat there trying to figure out how I could find a fork somewhere in the house and give myself a root canal to make the whole experience a little bit more pleasant. The four teens didn't utter a word. They were speechless after hearing all the graphic talk about the various health challenges. The rest of us periodically nodded and said, "Uh-huh," "Okay," and, "Then what did the doctor say?"

It was two hours of misery and gloom. As I suffered through it, I couldn't wait to get out of there and away from the discussion I really had no interest in. Am I exaggerating here? Maybe just a bit, but it is not far from the reality of that scene.

WE CAN ALL BE THAT WAY SOME DAY— OR MAYBE WE CAN TURN IT AROUND

We may all be in that position one day when medical issues are about all we have to talk about. (I hope that day is a long way away.) I left thinking I never wanted my grandkids to feel as uncomfortable around me in my home as those teens did sitting around listening to the shocking realities of getting old. Then I started thinking how I may make some people feel just as uncomfortable in other ways.

My grandkids tell me I'm always cleaning. My daughter tells me I need to learn how to relax with messiness at my home. My son-in-law tells me that I can't always have everything perfectly put away. My wife says I'm obsessive-compulsive. You know what? They're all correct in their assessments. I can make anyone feel uncomfortable because there is something in me that always cleans. Always.

Guests become paranoid whether they'll put their dishes or cups in the right place, and family is always concerned I'm watching to make sure everything is properly stowed. If someone is missing something, they come to me first. They know I've probably thrown it away if it was just sitting around.

I have to work hard to keep my need for cleaning and picking up clutter from getting in the way of relationships within my family. I can only imagine how many times my kids and grandkids have looked for one of their belongings because they put it in the wrong place. Well, to me it *was* the wrong place. So I felt compelled to move it to the right place. They had to get used to my idiosyncrasies.

Many times the way you want your home to be can keep your grandkids from being able to kick back and relax when they come visit. Your mission is truly to make your home their home. It should be a place of rest, a place to kick up their feet (yes, even on your pristine, glass-top coffee table sometimes) and consider it their second home.

Jesus said, "Come to me all who are weary and heavy laden and you will find *rest*." He didn't say, "Come to me and you will find a way to give yourself a root canal." He said *rest*. I can't think of any group of people who deserve a place to rest, a place of sanctuary, more than your grandkids. That's right. Not the grandparents. The grandkids. They go out and do battle every day against a world that works against what we all desire for their lives. They fight a contrary culture trying to steal their morals, values, faith, relationships, health, and peers. The least we can do is give them a place to recharge.

They're worn out. They're beat. They need a break. They need some rest. They need a retreat. They need a place where they are heard and listened to. They need a respite that refreshes and invigorates. They are looking for a safe harbor amid the storm where they can refuel and be understood. I hope your grandkids find that in their own home, but it's never a bad idea to be the backup plan, an extension of love and grace found in your—the grandparents'—home.

I want that to be your home. I hope you do too.

Let me ask you something. What do your grandkids feel when they walk in your front door? Is it a place where they find the rest they need, or is it a place where they are more worn out by the time they leave? Do they tell each other stories behind your back, quietly making fun of the way you do things? Is it a place of avoidance where you know everyone will only get along if there is no talk of politics or religion?

Will they bring their friends to meet you? What do they sense from you? Do they feel welcome? Is there always an open invitation? Would they spend the night with you? Do they sometimes just want to hang out with their grandparents?

There are a number of ways your home can provide a setting for physical, emotional, and spiritual rest. These include the setting you design, the atmosphere you create, the way you live between four walls, and the conversations your home invites. Let me explain.

Setting

I bet your grandkids would love to come to your home and find a place warm in relationship, relaxed in its furnishings, and welcoming to every weary and heavy-laden teen. Like a favorite restaurant, they long for a place where they can be catered to if you will.

I've walked into many a home where everything was in such order and so clean that it made me look messy! These homes feel like sterile environments that couldn't possibly allow the smallest amount of dirt or mess to enter its doors. I mean, no physical, literal mess or emotional and spiritual clutter. No controversial or messy talk would be allowed here. For teens, the welcome mat might as well say, "Don't Cross This Threshold."

I've walked into homes where families are so concerned about how everything looks on the outside that teens feel like their *dirty* insides better not come anywhere near it. Performance and appearance reign supreme, sometimes even at Grandpa and Granny's house. This kind of home is so concerned with how everything looks that little attention is paid to what's happening inside the heart. As long as grandkids look great on the outside, all is well, even if they're falling apart on the inside.

When they were young, you probably taught your grandkids to put away the games, toys, puzzles, and dolls they played with, right? Told them there is a place for everything and everything in its place, encouraged tidiness and supported the 1880's phrase *Cleanliness is next to godliness*. Admit it, did you ever tell your grandkids the myth that a messy room means you have an unorganized mind?

I found out the hard way that my desire to have everything clean, tidy, and in order in my home can, most times, create a barrier that stops them from wanting to be in our home. You would have thought I would have learned my lesson with my son when he was in the 8th grade. A true slob in my terms, somewhere I put the cleanliness of his room above the relationship that I had with him. I always found myself mad and disappointed that he didn't clean up his room and put his things away. I found myself quietly boiling when we sat down at the dinner table, knowing his room was a mess. He finally told me he would rather live somewhere else than live with me. It hit me like a ton of bricks when I realized my desire to have "everything in order" was more important than my own son.

It carried over to my first granddaughter who didn't quite like picking everything up after she spent a day with us. When she stated that she didn't want to come back to our house, I was blindsided that my desire for a home that's neat and tidy was really a barrier to a relationship that I longed for dearly. In all my desire to have everything in order, I was not creating a place of rest where people felt comfortable. I was creating a pristine environment that looked put together while I was destroying the chance to ever have a place of refuge for any of our family to ever want to be a part of.

Knowing what I know now, I would ask you the following:

Well, if your home is an extension of who you are, then what message is your home communicating to your grandkids? What message are your words communicating to your grandchildren? What phrases do you say the most with them? Are you sending a message that says they have to have their lives in order, put together, straightened up, clean, tidy, and everything in its place to be with you? Or do you give signals that your home and you are a safe harbor where your grandkids can be a mess, fall apart, and be less than altogether?

I think they prefer the latter because it offers a hand of hope. That kind of message says, "You can fall apart here; messes are welcome." Which message would appeal to your teen grandchild?

Hey, I know about cleaning and having everything in its place. Believe me. So I have to work hard to create a haven that welcomes anyone who is going through a tough time and in disarray. My wife has a pillow on our sofa that says it wonderfully, "A Beautiful Mess." She puts it there just to bug me, a hard-to-miss reminder to me to quit cleaning and holster your gun.

Atmosphere
The setting has more to do with the physical attributes of your home. The atmosphere has more to do with you. From the moment your grandkids knock on the front door to the time they drive off, you create the atmosphere.

Jan and I own a little place of rest in San Jose del Cabo, Mexico, where I am writing this book. It's our second home, a getaway from all the hustle and bustle of travel, speaking, and living with sixty high school kids. I love this place. I love the food. I love the activity. I love the beach. I love the people. I love it all, except for one thing—the way that people greet me within five minutes of getting out of the taxi. Someone inevitably asks when they can meet with me so they can sell me something or push their agenda on me. It grates me. It's not the way to start a relaxing time away from home.

When your grandkids walk in the door, who is the focus of attention? Their first interaction should not be about what you want or planned; it should be about them and what they want. Is your *agenda* to try to *sell* them one of the first things they face?

If you only see your grandkids a couple of times a year, might I suggest that before they enter your home, you have some type of communication throughout the year? That way, they know that you have an interest in them beyond a couple of weeks at Christmas or during the summer.

I'd like to suggest some ideas that might help create the atmosphere you want, to help them make your home a place where your grandkids want to park.

- Build a fire pit in your backyard and create a place for conversation (not lectures).
- Have a few good jokes to tell around the dinner table that will bring some belly laughs or tell some old stories that will bring people to tears.
- Get that larger flatscreen television and purchase whatever is needed to play some video games.
- Get a trampoline and put it in your backyard (for them, not you).
- Get a golf cart for your grandkids to drive around.
- Have plenty of board games to invoke fun and conversation (not *bored games* hated by all).
- Work on a thousand-piece jigsaw puzzle of a picture they like.
- Have a refrigerator full of their favorite foods.
- Get up early and have a wonderful breakfast awaiting them.

Don't let your music, your TV shows, your schedule, your favorite food, and your plans for games take over. Don't sit around and talk about your next medical procedure. This time is not about you. Remember, you only have so much time with your grandkids until you either kick the bucket or their calendar gets full and de-emphasizes your role in their life. You have one shot during the teen years as a grandma or grandpa. Make it count!

A word to the wise: Don't just have activities to fill the time. If your grandkids come over and you take them to a movie, remember they can see a movie anytime. They only get a small amount of time to see you. Make memories.

Above all, create an atmosphere where they know they are safe. A good friend of mine reminds me every time I see him that Jan and I are safe in his home. That is such a relief. It gives us permission to be ourselves, speak what is on our hearts, and share any concern or frustration that may be on our minds. It's an atmosphere that can only be created through relationship.

Rules of Operation

Okay, so I know many of you have read this far and probably think I advocate letting the crazies run the asylum. Just put the kids in charge and everything will be fine. You may think I promote just letting the grandkids come into your home and do whatever they want. Not at all. I believe in rules to construct the boundaries and limits, so all can function within a relational environment.

Grandkids need to understand what is allowed and what is not allowed in your home. These rules are necessary. You may even need to put up a small blackboard or sign that says, "Grandma's House Rules." When expectations are clearly stated, they can be correctly met. Everyone knows what's going to get them in trouble and what won't. Kids can still make either good choices or bad choices at that point, but they should know beforehand the limits and the consequences. Talk them out so you don't get taken advantage of when you can't hear or see them, or when you fall asleep before they do.

Here are the ways that I'd line out the expectations in our home:

First, In the Home
1. Everyone and everything will be treated with respect.
2. You are always welcome here. Anything illegal is not.
3. This home will be a safe place for all. Don't think you are the only one here.

Second, Your Cell Matters, So Do Your Manners
1. Bedtime is midnight. House is locked. TV, tablets, cell phones, game systems, laptops, and any other electronic devices are off.
2. No use of cell phones during mealtimes; video games limited to one hour.
3. No rudeness, crudeness, or nudeness, and don't kick our dog.
4. We can talk about anything; just keep it courteous.

Third, What Your Parents Can Expect from Us
1. We will share anything with your parents we think might be dangerous to you or others.

2. If your parents have different rules, we support and follow them unless they make an exception for your visit.

Fourth, What We Can Expect from You
1. We don't expect to be taken advantage of.
2. We don't owe you anything, but we want to give you everything.

Fifth, What You Can Expect from Us
1. You must understand there is nothing you can do to make us love you more, and there is nothing you can do to make us love you less.
2. Just like God.

Conversations Your Home Invites
Technology doesn't solve problems or create deeper relationships, conversation does. Good meals, a welcoming atmosphere, and a relational setting all work together so you can have conversations that offer opportunities to share your wisdom and give hope to your grandkids.

Another shift in the way grandparents should act is to allow a conversation that reveals the messiness of life, your life and theirs. You need to shift the focus from expecting excellence to allowing for failure. Welcome their imperfect selves and imperfect lives and their imperfect teen world to integrate with yours. Stop resonating perfection. They are old enough now to know nothing and no one is perfect. Anyone who expects perfection is a hypocrite or a fake.

Remember I mentioned earlier (in chapter 7) how a teen needs to be in the presence of imperfect people as they begin to realize and comprehend that their once-perfect world is just not anymore? Grasping this is tough. It's sad. And, yes, it's messy.

Making imperfection more comfortable is essential. The atmosphere creates the arena for change. You are the one to give permission for imperfection to be present. "For all have sinned and fall short . . ." (Romans 3:23, KJV) now becomes a reality. Teens can more than relate to what Paul wrote to the Romans when he said, "For I do not do the good I want to do, but the evil I do not want to do—this I keep on doing" (Romans 7:19).

This is not the time to be quoting to your teen grandchild, "Be perfect, therefore, as your heavenly Father is perfect" (Matthew 5:48). That will only discourage, not encourage.

Admitting imperfection is really pretty easy because you have never been perfect. No one is this side of heaven. Confession is the key. It makes you relatable to your teen grandkids. This should happen in the form of sharing stories of struggle, failure, disappointment, and hardship. Tell your grandkids when it was hard to forgive and easier to hate. Tell them how you handled it when someone picked on you. Tell them your biggest disappointments and what you later learned from them. Unfold the conversations at natural intervals, in short stories on walks, during games, in the car—not lectures but doing life together. Your imperfect conversations are essential to open the door for them to talk about their newly discovered imperfections.

Your words affirm their struggle and give them hope that they too can overcome the struggles and difficulties they face in their teen years and beyond. Your words help them identify with you. Your shared experiences connect you.

A young father of four once told me after attending one of our seminars that the day his dad admitted failure and showed himself to be imperfect was the day hope was ushered into his life.

I can tell you this for sure: Your grandchildren don't care as much about your accomplishments as your stories of disappointment. *Your accomplishments may motivate; your stories bring hope.*

So be careful of your words and how you come across. The setting, the atmosphere, and the rules of your home create a pathway for a conversation that is open and raw, vulnerable, and bonding. In his 1960 book *The Four Loves*, author C.S. Lewis lamented the opposite of such an atmosphere in families at times and affirmed the power of positive words from parents and grandparents alike.

We hear a great deal about the rudeness of the rising generation. I am an oldster myself and might be expected to take the oldsters' side, but in fact, I have been far more impressed by the bad manners of parents to children than by those of children to parents. Who has not been the embarrassed guest at family meals where the father or mother treated their grown-up offspring with an incivility which, offered to any other young people, would simply have terminated the acquaintance? Dogmatic assertions on matters which the children understand and their elders don't, ruthless interruptions, flat contradictions, ridicule of things the young take seriously sometimes of their religion insulting references to their friends, all provide an easy answer to the question, *Why are they always out? Why do they like every house better than their home?* Who does not prefer civility to barbarism?[11]

Your home will one day be silent. The chaos of kids and grandkids will be gone. Time moves on and so will your family. My hope for you is that everyone's memories of your home will be of rooms full of love, a kitchen overflowing with great scents, and walls that echo laughter. I hope your home is a place of fun, hope, relaxation, and safe harbor for grandkids who know that they know that they know your deep love for each of them.

— PART V —

A LEGACY
THEY'LL NEVER
FORGET

Chapter 21

SUPPORTING YOUR KIDS...AND THEN THEIR KIDS...IN WORD AND DEED

And let us consider how we may spur one another

on toward love and good deeds.

Hebrews 10:24 (NIV)

Perhaps like you, I always thought I was a pretty good parent. I attended every event possible, loved my kids, provided what was needed, and made sure they survived their toddler and teen years. When I became a grandparent, my instinct was to do the same things I had done well in my parenting years.

There isn't a grandparent out there who wouldn't support the concept that kids need a parent, not another friend. And there isn't a parent out there who wouldn't support the notion that grandchildren need grandparents, not another parent.

THAT IMAGINARY BOUNDARY FOR GRANDPARENTS

The minute a grandparent crosses the imaginary boundary that divides the roles of parents and grandparents, they violate basic principles of family structure. Grandparents who act like the parents when the parents are right there in the picture cause confusion and conflict. Eventually the power struggle between the two generations divides families.

There are situations where grandparents must intervene and some-times take over. That occurs when physical, medical, legal, or mental issues incapacitate their children, or when death, drugs, or divorce have created an unsafe atmosphere for their grandkids. I know many dear grandmas and grandpas who have to parent the second genera-tion. While I don't think they would choose to be in that position, they willingly assume the role of sacrifice to provide a better life for their grandkids.

I would eagerly and gladly shoulder the parental role should my grandchildren's parents (my kids) become debilitated, disabled, or unwilling to parent for some reason. I'd assume this role, but it wouldn't be a position I would choose. It's family so I would accept and embrace it. Because they are my grandkids, I would do anything to help.

That responsibility in the face of adversity is far different than what I mean here. I'm talking about well-meaning grandparents who step in where they're not needed or wanted by acting more like a parent than a grandparent to their grandchildren. I'm talking about grandparents who undermine their daughter or son because they think they can do a better job or feel like the parents aren't accomplishing what is needed in raising their grandkids.

I never had a grandparent involved in my life so I wasn't quite sure what my role was supposed to be when I became one. I never had an uncle involved in my life; that's why I'm probably not a good uncle. I'm not altogether sure what role they play in a family. Since I had no grandparent to model myself after when I became a grandparent, I had to figure out quickly what my new role would be. Being a grandparent doesn't mean I parent my grandkids grandly or on a greater scale. It means I have a new role that has something to offer of grander proportions.

When grandparents complement and assist what parents are charged by God with doing, the tide for teens can turn.

GRANDPARENTS HAVE THE POWER

Grandparents possess the power of influence in the lives of their grandchild, but it hurts, not helps, if they wield that power by trying to be the parent. Undermining parents drives a wedge between you and your kids. That wedge then divides you from your grandchildren. You can help shape your grandchildren, but only by coming alongside their parents.

If you only offer the role of a parent, then your grandkids will never have the opportunity to benefit from the presence of grandparents in their lives. If you've never been a grandparent before and you don't know how, don't assume it's just a continuation of your parenting skills and capabilities. It's a completely different role.

Some grandparents want to prove something to their kids, so they try to make up through their grandkids whatever they missed or messed up during their parenting years. In their eyes, all can be made right by grandparenting like a parent. They can right past wrongs by pouring their misguided parenting energies into their grandkids. It doesn't work.

You may have to accept the fact that maybe you weren't a great parent. Grandchildren do not offer you the chance to redeem yourself in that department. Remember, it's not about you.

When I think about how I really was while my kids were growing up, sometimes I think we were all just trying to survive. School, work, ministry, more work, time away from home, and never enough money. Those were hard years spent mostly trying to keep everything together. I think I landed on the borderline between being an okay parent and a good parent. I'm not sure I ever hit pretty good.

I warn you now and will share more points later. The minute you begin to contradict, undermine, or bad-mouth your kids (your grand-kids' parents), either by word or by action, you cause more problems than you fix.

I've seen this story hundreds of times. A grandparent believes that a mom or dad isn't handling the kids (their grandkids) in an appropriate way. The grandparent then stops supporting the parents and offers to help, telling the grandkids they can move in—against the mom's or dad's desire. It sets up a dynamic very similar to co-parenting after divorce, where loyalties are divided, and children can manipulate everyone involved. No one wins when there is competition amongst the primary adult figures in a teen's life. A good guy/bad guy dynamic develops, with frustrated parents and misguided grandparents.

TIMES FOR COOLING OFF WITH THE GRANDPARENTS

Now, I think there are times when a cooling-off period is needed between parents and teens, and the decision to have a child stay with grandma and grandpa for a time may be a good thing. It's good only when the parents and grandparents are on the same page so the already struggling teen can't play one side against the other and get away with murder. It is not a good thing if the grandparents don't or won't support the parents.

I recall one family in particular. A mother was having a tough time with her son because the teen had such a winning personality that he had become quite the con artist. This was a side of their grandson the grandparents had never seen. The parents decided on a course of action to help bring their son back in line with their family principles. Of course, the son balked at the idea of having to make changes in his life and complained in his best winning manner to the higher ups—his grandparents. As well intended as could be but without consulting the parents, they offered their grandson a chance to come live with them. Big no-no. The grandson now had a way out and no longer had to make changes in his life. And the grandparents couldn't see what was going on by their loving grandson as he conned them and nearly ruined the family in the process.

Mom and dad felt invalidated. The son got out of assuming responsibility, and the grandparents' offer built a wall in the relationships within the family. Providing for their grandson quickly turned into enabling. The grandson in his new environment was able to continue his foolish behavior. Honestly, the grandson was lucky he didn't lose his life. His grandparents' good intentions merely extended this young man's walk on the wild side.

CAN GRANDPARENTS BE BETTER PARENTS OF THE GRANDKIDS?

Can grandparents do a better job than parents in raising the grandkids? Well, sure they can. I know I can. Grandparents have prior experience. They can repeat their successes and have learned from their mistakes. In their day, kids *knew better* than to behave like their grandkids might be behaving, and they believe they can nip those behaviors right in the bud.

Grandparents must be doing an awesome job because all I see on their Facebook walls and in annual Christmas cards are the wonderful pictures they post and send of everyone all smiles and full of laughter. For the most part, a grandparent's role is to be the fun guy (or gal). They don't have to and should not deal with all the mess.

What I don't see in these happy photos are the everyday interactions where conflicts, confrontations, disagreements, fights, struggles over homework, poor choices, completing chores, and little skirmishes on the battlefront of family life are the reality. These paint a better and much more accurate picture of a home intent on helping teens get through their adolescent years alive and with some measure of relationship intact when a child reaches maturity.

In the case mentioned earlier, the grandparents eventually saw the light, the same one the parents had seen for months, and they then became a part of the solution rather than adding to the present problems. They got on board with the parents and presented a united front to their grandson so he couldn't maneuver around any of them. These wiser grandparents now supported the parents even if they didn't agree with their methods, their style, or their requests for their child. They assumed their rightful place of being the grandparents they needed to be.

If your kids come to you and ask for help when they are struggling with your grandkids, that's a different story. In that scenario, grandparents are being invited to be involved in the process of helping when all parental efforts have been exhausted. Grandparents may then take on a short-term, more parental role in the life of the struggling grandchild, but it's with the parents' consent. Everyone is on the same page, so there's no wiggle room for the teen's rebellion to grow. There's a far different attitude about grandparents' involvement when they have been issued an invitation by the parents, rather than barging their way in.

Your home may be a haven for your grandkids, but that doesn't mean it's a free-for-all for selfish behavior. When my grandkids come to my home, there are home rules. However, if they violate the home rules, I am limited in my authority to dole out consequences. If a grandchild breaks one of the house boundaries, grandparents don't usually have the authority to ground a child, take away their car, or park their cell phone for a few days. At least not without asking the parents' permission first.

Grandparents do have the authority to either report the infraction to parents (especially in the earlier years of a grandchild's life) or tell grandkids they are welcome in their home as long as certain rules are adhered to. You don't have to be used and abused by anyone. My suggestion for you is to require respect, honesty, and obedience conveyed on pictures, placards, and signs hanging on your walls and talked about around your dinner table. Say things such as the following:

> *"Hey, I want you to know that we honor respect as a strength, as most disrespect comes from a place of weakness."*
>
> *"Guys, above anything else my hope is that you will always be full of honesty. Telling the truth sometimes hurts people but being dishonest to people will only hurt them deeper."*
>
> *"Hey, listen up. I'm not asking for much, but I am asking you trust me on this one and be in obedience to what I'm saying, even if you don't agree with me."*

When you communicate these principles, you do so as a grandparent. Your appeal to them relies on the strong relationships you develop with them. Present your principles in the form of short lessons, bits of wisdom, and traits you hope they pick up from you while in your presence.

SPEAKING FROM THE OUTSIDE

By supporting your son or daughter as the parent, you use your influence as one who is speaking from the outside. This is really a position of strength, as you don't have to correct. In reality, you don't have to be involved in the lives of your grandchildren at all. You choose to do so. This shows your grandchildren you want to be in a special relationship with them. No one can make you. It's your choice. When they see this, it gives you a voice they won't find elsewhere.

When you support your grandkids' parents, they will be more apt to come ask for help and seek your counsel. You will be seen as participating teammates rather than adversarial foes, thus giving you more of a say in the lives of your grandkids and a stronger relationship with your adult kids.

THE RULES OF THE ROAD

When you think your kids have it wrong when it comes to your grandkids, here's what you can do right.

Don't Parent when You're Not the Parent; Be the Grandparent

I don't agree with every way my kids parent their children. There are many times I think I'd have even better grandkids if their parents would just follow my line of thought. I've had my tongue replaced twice as I've bitten it so many times wanting to suggest a better way. After all, I write books and speak on this stuff every day.

Then I remember the parenting gig is all theirs. Not mine. I had my turn. Yes, I think they're on their iPads and cell phones too much. Yes, they should get those kids out of diapers and quit sticking that pacifier plug in their mouth. Yes, they shouldn't say certain words around them. Yes, they should push them in some areas and quit pushing so hard in others. Yes, they should make them clean up more and quit making messes. Yes, they should help them understand how great we are as grandparents. All the "Yeses," in my mind, should remain there. In my mind, and not be pushed on my kids (my grandkid's parents), because it's not about me, it's about helping my kids be the best parents to my grandkids without me pushing my personal agenda of what I think might be best.

They just don't do this parenting thing as I did and would do again. The reason? Because God placed my grandkids in my kids' care to parent, not in mine. He gave me kids to parent, and if I did such a great job then why don't I trust my kids to repeat it now with my grandkids? Ultimately,

I do trust them. We just do things differently. So I'll keep my mouth shut, keep biting my tongue, and trust that God knows what He's doing. And I'll pray He helps me become the grandparent He's created me to be.

Support Your Kid's Parenting Styles and Desires
Styles will always be different. Your kids say the same thing all of us have said, "I don't want to parent my kids the way my parents parented me." They're doing it differently because they learned some things from you that they don't want to carry on.

Just as you are trying to honor the position God placed you in, they are honoring the position He put them in. Maybe God is encouraging your kids to raise their kids in a certain way. Be careful. Your lack of support may actually be a lack of support for God's plan for their lives.

You need to do your thing and do it well. Let your kids do theirs with all your support.

Don't undercut your kids.

Support Your Kids Even in Your Disagreement
This may mean you help your grandchild understand your role by saying, "Even though I don't agree with your mom, I do support her. I always have, and I always will. You guys need to work this one out, and I'll help where I can. However, I won't go against what she says."

Offer a Place of Relief and Rest, Not Escape
Offer that place of rest where they feel safe and can be refreshed and rekindled, but not a place where they escape the consequences of their behavior or elude and avoid the responsibilities put on them. At any age, a child would much rather avoid a painful situation. I encourage you to provide a place where they don't avoid the pain of life but learn to navigate through the agony and heartache of growing up.

Give Advice Only When Asked
Even a fool appears wise when he keeps his mouth shut. Have you read that a few times throughout this book? It's a wise proverb that bears repeating, and repeating, and repeating some more.

Don't Bad-mouth by Words or Actions

Let your grandkids know of your own parental struggles. Make your kids (their parents) appear normal, not as villains. Don't do anything in secret except for surprise birthday parties and anniversary celebrations. The minute you say, "Don't tell your mom this," or "Don't let your dad know," you are bad-mouthing their parents. You are not respecting their positions. You are showing you don't have to give your support. Sometimes your actions speak louder than words.

Send Your Kids and Their Kids on a Vacation to Spend Time Together Without You

It's fun to spend time with grandkids, but I encourage you to help your kids make some memories with your grandkids as well. Give them fun times away from your presence.

While you want to communicate and you want to share with your grandchildren, don't ever forget whose kids they really are. You have been given a chance to be involved in the lives of these teens who don't belong to you. It's a blessing! You get to participate in the fun without all the dirty work anymore. You know what? I enjoy my grandkids, and I never changed one of their diapers. When they get sick, I let them go throw up somewhere else. When they're in trouble, they get to answer to someone else. When they pull some stupid stunt, it's all on their parents. I get to sit back and enjoy the good times; parents have to deal with all the rotten stuff.

So try to give them a break from the day in, day out routine. Help them enjoy their kids and have some fun. It's easy for grandparents to be a killjoy of fun within the family if the fun is all about having it around grandparents. Show your support for your kids by blessing them and granting them the opportunity to spend some time as a family and make some great memories.

Don't Ever Believe You Know Best Because You Don't

You don't live with the struggling grandchild every day. You may not be able to detect bluffing behavior during occasional visits. Your grandkids may be sweet as honey to you and be a living nightmare for mom or dad. Your grandkids' parents need your support, not abandonment or criticism.

You are to give a bigger-picture view, yes. You are to give perspective. But that doesn't mean you see everything happening. I hear parents mention to me all the time that their parents would never understand because they don't see the half of it and wouldn't believe it if they did. As mentioned before, I can change spark plugs in a car but I can't replace the engine. I'm not the expert on that engine. I simply don't see the whole picture of how everything works, connects, and functions together properly. You may see a little, but that doesn't mean you understand it all. Don't charge in as an expert. Go to your kids in humility, offering to listen and be available to answer anything they ask. Remember, you're not living with your grandkids, so there's a lot you don't know. Supporting your grandkid's parents may just be the best way to support your grandkids. Let them know that they're the best, even when you think you are better.

Chapter 22

MAKING MEMORIES
BEFORE YOU
LOSE YOURS

And I will make every effort to see that after my departure

you will always be able to remember these things.

2 PETER 1:15 (NIV)

The question that looms for many grandparents in their time of reflection is, "What do I want to be known for?" Maybe the more important question is, "How will they remember me?" It's not necessarily what you want to be known for that counts, but how they will recount their times with you.

MAKING MEMORIES WITH MONEY

One of my greatest fears is that when I die, the money I saved and invested will be distributed to my family, and I didn't get to spend it on creating experiences while I was with them. I don't want to miss these moments because I am too darn busy. Money sure hasn't been my focus, but I saved diligently so Jan and I would be taken care of in our later years. Now I'm more concerned with the memories in my family's hearts than I am the amount of money in my bank account.

I was recently reminded of the futility of gathering and collecting everything we do in life, knowing that none of it can be taken with us when we die. I attended the funeral of my dear friend David Muth after he succumbed to his fight with Parkinson's. I arrived in Indiana for his funeral and walked in after the service began. I was ushered to the front to sit with his wife and daughters. I sat through the service holding the hands of his girls and looking at him in the casket. As I walked up to see my friend, I noticed that his wife Amy had put memorabilia of sorts in the casket propped up around David—pictures of times together, items that stirred memories with this wonderful man, and a few trinkets that meant nothing to most, yet were invaluable to the family. It was touching, to say the least, and my eyes kept dripping on the casket as I recalled the wonderful times we had together.

What was not there in the casket was money. No cash, no checkbook, nor were there any pictures of dollar bills. No car, no valuable possessions were being buried with him. When we loaded him up for the graveside, there was no U-Haul attached to his hearse. Just him and the beautiful memories he created for his family.

If you can't take any of it with you, then spend it on experiences that last a lifetime and leave a legacy. Spend times together that bind the hearts in relationship together. This crazy disease took away David's time here on earth, but it couldn't take away his family's beautiful memories of their times together. Though painful to remember, those memories are, and always will be, wonderfully inscribed on the hearts of those he loved.

Money is a great inheritance. It's a bonus, a gift, a blessing from left field, usually not anticipated and always greatly appreciated. However, why wait until you're gone to share a little of it?

I was reminded of how a little went a long way when I gave my granddaughter twenty dollars to support a car wash that she was participating in. She was so grateful and excited that I helped. A simple twenty-dollar bill…that's all it took to let her know I cared about what she cared about. For me, it was a reminder to her that when she needs something, I want her to come to me to ask. That doesn't keep her from going to her own parents or others she knows, but it affirms our relationship in a way that will keep her coming back for more than just money.

One of these days, I'm going to write checks for ten thousand dollars and give one to each of my grandkids. It's one of my goals. It is founded on a wish I had that was never fulfilled. When Jan and I were first married, we had no money. We struggled to make ends meet. It was a great date night if we were able to air-pop some popcorn and sit and watch a movie. I painted apartments in the evening, cleaned toilets, unclogged drains, worked two jobs, and was ecstatic when Young Life decided to pay me twenty-five dollars a month as I volunteered.

At one point, I remember we had a health insurance payment due of twenty-two dollars. I took my high school ring to a pawnshop and got twenty-three dollars for it. I paid the bill and ended up with one dollar in my pocket. I remember thinking, *I just wish someone would help us in some way.* We had a baby due, I was a student at Tulsa University, and Jan dropped out of nursing school because of morning sickness.

That's when I said to myself, *One of these days, I'm going to give some money to my grandkids at just the right time.* Now I'm thinking, *Why not?* I might as well give it to them while I'm alive and enjoy their excitement and pleasure than wait until I'm gone and everything is divvied up among my heirs anyway. Here's the only catch I'll put with the money. Each of my grandkids will be charged with giving the same amount to their own grandchildren one day when those grandkids need it the most. It's kind of a pay-it-forward deal, the start of a new tradition for our family.

Chances are, by the time my kids get my inheritance, they really won't need it. They'll be making their own living and making ends meet. But unexpected windfalls give you the chance to do things, go places, or experience something you might not budget for otherwise. If I can give them that joy, why not give it now?

The inheritance you leave is about more than dollars; it's about leaving an impact on your grandkids. Events and occasions that trigger memories are important. These open the door to the life skills you shared, the legacy you built in their lives, and remind them of the special relationship you had with them.

When your grandchildren remember you, what will they remember you for?

The experiences with you are important. They open the doors to the hearts of your grandchild. My family has wonderful memories of going to the beach. After I'm buried or burnt, I hope that every time my family is at the beach they remember my love for the ocean, the wind, the waves, and the sea life we all enjoyed watching together. Those are great memories, but I want them to recall more than just, *Hey, remember how Poppa loved the beach?*

My wife Jan has populated East Texas with birds, as she feeds them every day. We have every type of bird you can imagine darting in and out of our backyard on a daily basis. Friends give her bird towels, bird glasses, bird gifts, and bird emblems. She's known as the bird lady. If that's all she's known as, that's kind of weird. If people think of Jan when they see a bird and remember nothing else about her, then her legacy will pass quickly and soon be forgotten.

But I think Jan is creating much more of a legacy. I think when friends and loved ones see birds, they will think of Jan. When they think of her and the memories they have of her, they'll also remember her love of animals, her ability to talk to anyone, her fun-loving personality, her strength through pain, her ability to listen well, her efforts to make everyone's life better, the lessons she taught, her love for God, and her ability to share how she found so much in Him. They'll think about how she laughed in the face of conflict, how she gave generously, and how her words were full of wisdom. They'll remember all of these things because even a bunch of feathery friends stir memories of deeper connections of who she really was to others.

Do you have memories built up in the hearts of your grandkids that will remind them of you? It's never too late to start.

Twenty years ago I had this crazy idea to pile up all the Christmas trees from all the houses at Heartlight and burn them on New Year's Eve. The next year we stuffed some fireworks in the trees. The following year we added gasoline. Every year, the blaze gets bigger and bigger. This family tradition has now turned into a community event. People come from everywhere to see the Christmas tree burning at the Gregston's place. It's a memory that will be with our family for years.

Now, I'm not suggesting you do the same. I don't know where you live, and you might get in trouble doing something in the city we habitually do in the country. I do suggest you create something memorable, magnificent, and meaningful to your family.

What smells remind your grandkids of you? Is it that special candle you always burn, the perfume or cologne you wear, or the smell of your cooking at various times of the year? Whenever I smell boiling shrimp, I think of my dad. Is there a smell that is just unique to your home that reminds them of you? We had a young lady at Heartlight a couple of years ago who made a statement reflecting on her memory of home. She said she would occasionally go into her closet and open up her suitcase so she could *get a whiff of home*. The scent reminded her of what she missed dearly.

Start some traditions around your home. Perhaps it is leaving a jigsaw puzzle on the dining room table for everyone to gather and piece together. Maybe it's nights around the fireplace where everyone just catches up. Have you thought of having a joke night around the dinner table every Saturday night? Popping a champagne bottle on New Year's Eve? Or eating a special cultural meal to remind you of your heritage?

What is unique about you that you could teach your grandchild? Do you play a musical instrument? If so, purchase one for your grandchild and help them learn. Teach them how to do carpentry, operate a tractor, use some tools, build something, repair fence line, or care for and feed some animals. (Can you tell we live in the country?) Find one of your skills and talents and teach it to another.

Find a lifelong sport or activity you can do with your grandchild. I'm talking about golf, tennis, horseback riding, weight lifting or working out, shooting guns at a gun range, hunting, or any activity that can be done throughout the rest of your grandkids' lives. Schedule a time to go on a mission trip with your grandchild or volunteer somewhere local on a regular basis together. Go somewhere they'll go with no one else and keep a laid-back schedule that isn't filled with constant activity, so you have plenty of time for personal interaction.

Take a vacation and invite the whole family. When you go, eat a special meal that second night (after all have rested up) and share with them the beauty of family and how you want this trip to be an annual event.

Take a grandchild or two to an event that wows them, a concert of a favorite artist, a backstage experience, a Broadway musical, or a big sports event.

My granddaughter Maile is a lover of country music. She and I have gone to the Country Music Awards almost every year for eight years. We even attended the CMA Festival in Nashville one year, and I let her bring a couple of her friends. One night months later, her friends came over to our home and they started asking questions about marriage. They asked me what I looked for in the gal I'd married, Maile's grandmother. This moment was years in the making and gave the opportunity of a lifetime to share with her, at her request, the wisdom I had gathered throughout my 46 years or marriage. And it all began because we connected through our love of country music. My prayer is that we'll be able to make this annual pilgrimage to this event for as long as I am able. I can't afford it. But I can't afford not to.

Where would your granddaughter or grandson love to go? Why not make plans to take them?

What do you do on special holidays? Is there a ritual around your home? Is there a tradition to eat a Thanksgiving meal and then watch football or soccer all afternoon? Do you go to a Christmas Eve service, come home and open presents, and then spend Christmas afternoon going to a newly released movie?

If your grandkids only occasionally visit, make sure you have some things lined up for activities. As they get older, plan on some time where all can sit around and talk—not just be entertained. Go horseback riding, take a walk on the beach, ride ATV's around somewhere, shoot skeet in someone's field, or go to the symphony or a play and then out to eat.

Plan a fishing or hunting trip of a lifetime or a shopping spree in a place your grandkids have never been. Go to a tropical island or take that trip to Disney World you've always wanted to take. If you can't go, send others so they can have a wonderful experience.

Do something special on birthdays, the beginning of school, graduations, and weddings. Make it special by your attendance, but also provide something for those events that makes them—and your participation in them—memorable.

Spend time around a fireplace or an open fire on a cold night, whether it is in your backyard, on a beach, or on a mountaintop. Make it special.

Have a week where you entertain the grandkids when they come spend time with you. Make those memories by cooking great meals and wearing you out showing them they are special. When you can no longer do that at your home, go someplace else to make it happen.

These are all memory makers that will bring you to mind. When you're gone and there is a trigger that reminds them of you, it will prompt them to recall the loving impact you had on their life.

Personally, I love the idea and thought that my grandkids will remember me every time they smell the burning of powder and see the beauty of rockets, explosives, and fireworks. I'm sure those will bring a smile to their faces as they remember all the times we burnt up some Christmas trees and ushered in the New Year.

But that's not the only thing I want them to remember about me. I want that memory and other memories of me to remind them of the wisdom I shared along the way. I want them to recall and put to good use in their lives the particular and specific nuggets of truth demonstrated and lived out by the way I treated them and the way they saw me treat other people.

Make some memories before you lose yours.

The remembrance of your generosity and kindness will last many lifetimes.

Yes, memories of you will last. Make sure they are good ones. This is the time of life to make sure all unfinished business gets taken care of. Is there something hidden in your closet? Are there skeletons that might come out after you pass away that could taint the memories of your good times together with your family? Is anything currently unresolved between you and any family members? Come clean and take care of the business of forgiveness and making amends now.

Don't leave your family hurting, wishing things could have been different, and talking about you negatively later. Is there something you are hiding about yourself from others? Could there be some unspoken pain that, if brought out in the open, would help everyone understand why things are the way they are? Are there habits, past or present, which need to be addressed so there are no surprises after you're gone? Are you fearful about some things in your past that you really don't think God is big enough to handle? God's Word tells us that's just not true.

Even to your old age and gray hairs I am he, I am he who will sustain you. I have made you and I will carry you; I will sustain you and I will rescue you. (ISAIAH 46:4)

I encourage you to leave this world with a clean slate. Tell it all, my friend. Tell it all. Tell the truth, the whole truth, and nothing but the truth. Make sure that no word can be said about you that is contrary to what everyone already knows, so your legacy will not be stained by something you left hidden during your life that is discovered after you're gone.

Those conversations are hard, but they are essential to a legacy that is spotless and unblemished. They might begin like this:

Your grandmother and I have something to tell you.
I want you to know that I'm not perfect.
There are some things in my life you don't know about.
I don't want you to hear these things from anyone else.
I've been to some places and done some things you don't know about.
There are some things in our family I want you to know about so
    they go no further.
Knowing what I know may help you see things in a different light.
I want you to know I haven't been totally honest with you.
I didn't get to where I am without making some mistakes along
    the way.
Poor choices haunted me earlier in life; I don't want you to make
    the same mistakes.

Clear the air, admit wrongdoings, ask for forgiveness, and strive to make your relationships right.

Many fear that the admission of wrongdoing will ruin a legacy and stain a memory beyond repair. Quite the contrary. What you will do by admitting your mistakes and failures is give your family members permission to clean out theirs. Through this, you usher in a world of hope for your grandkids and freedom in your family. You lay the groundwork for mental, emotional, and spiritual health. They'll remember the fun times, but also your admission of wrongdoing will be burned in their hearts forever. Not in a way that taints their memory of you, but in a way that causes them to remember your strength of character. Funny, isn't it? The hope will be ushered into the lives of your grandchildren not through your perfection, but through your imperfections.

They will remember you in the following ways:

Remember when Grandpa shared about his life and let us know we, too, can make it?

Remember when Grandma admitted her problem with anger and let us know why that existed in her life?

Remember when Grandpa told us the truth about our family?

Remember when Grandma shared with us how important it is not to hide anything?

Remember when Grandpa cried and shared about his hurt and his poor choices?

Remember when Grandma told us what really happened?

Remember when Grandma and Grandpa gave us all hope and let us know that we're all going to be okay?

Go make memories before you lose yours. Leave a legacy of hope and influence.

Chapter 23

WHEN LIFE GIVES YOU A MULLIGAN AND THE CHANCE TO MAKE IT RIGHT

Forgetting what is behind and straining toward what is ahead,

I press on toward the goal to win the prize for which God

has called me heavenward in Christ Jesus.

PHILIPPIANS 3:13-14 (NIV)

*I*n recent years I notice that I know many more of the celebrities who die each year. When year-end memorials roll around, I'm surprised at how many of them I remember. When people from *your era* start dropping right and left, a friend reminded me it's a sign your time on this earth may be coming to a close. So I decided I would just quit watching all those end-of-the-year memorials.

Country singer Rory Feek and I were sitting one time at the George Jones Memorial concert in Nashville watching all the old-timey, famous-but-aging country artists get up and sing George Jones songs as a tribute to him. It was remarkable—but not in a good way—because they didn't sound so good anymore. And it was evident they were in that season of life where gravity had somewhat taken over. Rory said, "It's a reminder that we're all going to be there."

If you're reading this book, you know quite a few folks in those *In Memory* reels. Use those reminders to spur you on, not to focus on where you're headed but to determine to deposit everything you can in those you leave behind here.

PARENTS INFLUENCE, GRANDPARENTS LEAVE A LEGACY

I encourage you to make sure the legacy you're leaving is intended to meet the needs in your grandkids' lives. Don't try to cram in activities and speeches with a goal of making sure you're remembered. That's not your priority. Your priority is to invest so many important things in the lives of your family members that they can't help but remember you every time they turn around. Make sure your motivation is about meeting needs in your family, especially when your investment is desperately needed in the life of your teen grandkids.

The beauty of grandparenting is that it gives you a do-over, a mulligan, where you get to drop the ball and take another swing. You can choose to make things right in order to highlight yourself, or you can make things right because you acknowledge you missed the mark sometimes in your own parenting years.

Quite honestly, I believe one way you can love your kids is by loving their kids well. Show your kids you are willing to do for their kids what you missed doing with them. Acknowledge where you blew it, accept responsibility, and ask them for the chance to make it right. There's something pretty cool about a second chance or another opportunity to do what you didn't do before.

What I have found is that the grandparents who leave a legacy of influence and hope for their grandchildren are usually servants. They give generously, extend grace, exude gratefulness, and desire to be involved in their family. They demonstrate genuine and authentic love for each member. History and our grandkids will judge us by the wisdom of our actions, not just our words. They are watching how we treat people, how we help others, and how we serve the Lord.

I want a do-over. I desire a second chance. I want to fill in the gaps I created when I was trying to parent and survive life's challenges at the same time and felt like I didn't do either very well at times. I really do want to right some wrongs, correct some mistakes, and take the wisdom I've discovered through the years and apply it to my family.

A man I was acquainted with more than forty years ago recently passed away, and as I read the tributes his grandkids wrote about him, I was amazed at how he impacted their lives. I also remembered how he impacted mine. Dave Tillack spoke into my life by reminding me to consider others more highly than myself. But he said it in a whole new way to me, one I shared with you in these pages. It bears repeating.

In other words, we're called to be servants of the Real King. Why would we want to lower ourselves to be some carpetbagger Ruler?

That is exactly how Dave lived his life. He was a servant to all, especially to his grandkids. Their lives are forever changed because of Dave's influence. This guy did it right. He is a great example of one who has passed on a legacy of hope. If half of what was said about this man is ever said about me, then I will leave twice the legacy of influence I ever thought I could.

People will forget how you look, but they won't forget how you made them feel.

Dave's impact ran deep, but it didn't develop overnight. I first met Dave and his wife, Sue, forty years ago when I was a young youth minister in Tulsa. Dave was forty years old at the time and wanted to teach a Sunday School class of eighth graders. I told him it was all his. His three kids grew up in the youth group and are now the dearest parents and grandparents. I know this because of the tributes they posted to their grandfather Dave. The legacy he left clearly lives on in them.

Dave's grandson Duncan is a twenty-five-year-old medical student who posted the following on Facebook:

"Grandad, thanks for making your love for everyone so clear and for always telling me that you were proud of me, even when I was doing nothing to be proud of. You told me to always know the color of my patient's eyes once I am a doctor, not just look down at the screen, and I hope I can do that. Thanks for always being so sweet to my wife, Alex. I'm glad that you got to meet sweet Lively, our daughter. I'll see you again some day, but in the meantime, I'll do my best to keep making you proud. Love you."

When I spoke to Duncan, he stated his granddad was one of the most selfless people he ever met. He poured his life into others. He even joked that Grandad would wear the same clothes every day because he never thought of buying new ones for himself and would want to provide for others anyway.

A common theme that ran through my conversations with all of Dave's grandkids went a lot like this:

"He was always proud of me, and he would let you know it," Duncan said.

To Duncan, Dave was like a second dad, willing to go catch crawdads down by the creek, and always calling and catching up to find out what was going on in his life. When Dave died, Duncan shared that his granddad's life was the perfect book, and his last chapter showed everyone how to leave this earth the same way he lived.

"Grandad reconciled everything, called those he needed to call, and checked off all the boxes. I miss him dearly," Duncan said.

Grandson Tanner posted this:

"Anyone who knew my granddad knew that he was incredibly selfless and put God above and before everything else. He was always looking for ways to help and serve even if it was inconvenient or caused him pain. Looking back at the last 22 years, I can only wish I would have called him even more to hear him answer the phone with, 'Is that my sweet boy,' listened to more of his stories, appreciated his wisdom and encouragement, and asked more questions. The loss of someone you love is never easy, but to have hope in the Lord and knowing that we will all be reunited makes it that much sweeter. I pray I can be a man of God like you were and be the type of person that would make you proud. I love you, Grandad!"

Tanner told me how Dave was intentional about everything he did. He mentioned how his grandad would catch crickets and crawdads. (Evidently Dave had this thing for catching bugs or was just desperate to find a way to connect with his grandkids. Ha!) What he remembers most is, "how my grandad prayed with us and for us." He said Dave wouldn't just call to ask questions but called to be involved in their lives. Interestingly, Tanner mentioned that his grandad was always concerned that one day he would not be relevant in others' lives. Tanner assured me that Dave remained relevant and remembered as a listener and one who constantly encouraged.

Granddaughter Caroline, a senior in high school, told me this:

"My grandad wasn't like someone who just stopped in twice a year and gave us gifts. He knew about everything and would pray for us and celebrate with us in any accomplishment we attained," she said. "He adapted himself to my circumstances, even taught me how to serve overhand, and was one time my cheerleading coach. Can you believe that? My grandad, teaching cheers to a bunch of girls and showing us how to build a pyramid! As clueless as he was about cheerleading, he was so determined to have an impact on each our lives. He was clueless but wanted to have a role in your life."

She added that he had a *blunt love,* telling her once, "Caroline, you don't have to play basketball. You're not good at it." She mentioned that he never wanted to be a burden to any of them and would always say at the end of a phone call, "Okay, I'll let you get back to your life."

"He would always tell me how proud he was of me. I was there when he took his last breath and I wanted him to know how proud I was of him, having such an impact on so many people and now dying without any regrets or anybody to reconcile with," Caroline said.

Dave's college-age grandson Keaton said a memorable time he had with his grandad centered around handing him tools to finish out a basement in their new home.

"Grandad said, 'You're the anticipator, always handing me what I needed before I knew I did.' That was important to me," Keaton said.

He, too, mentioned that his grandad was blunt. Dave wasn't shy about saying things that needed to be said, but always with a laugh and smile on his face.

Granddaughter Abigail wrote this on her Facebook post:

"Rest in peace to the best grandfather I ever could have asked for. No words can describe how much I love you and how grateful I am for the many things you taught me and the love you gave me. I thank God He gave me these past 20 years full of memories that will last me the rest of my life. You were such a huge part of my world. See you soon, handsome."

Another granddaughter, Katie, wrote,

"Today I lost my grandad. He brought me into his arms when I was trying so hard to push everyone away. He always knew my potential and pushed me when I thought everything was too far out of reach. He gave me unconditional love and only ever judged me for my hair color. I miss both of my grandparents, but I am so thankful to meet people every day who love them as much as I do. I hope to carry that love and guidance with me every day so their legacy can live on through me."

Granddaughter Emily wrote,

"Miss you, my sweet boy. I can't wait to live my life serving others like you. Thank you for being my most loving, patient listening ear. I will forever miss your perfect answers to my endless questions. I'll be seeing you, xoxo."

Dave played a unique role in each of his grandkids' lives, always adapting new strategies to make deeper connections. If that meant getting down in the mud catching crawdads and crickets or waving streamers coaching a handful of cheerleaders, Dave engaged eagerly and did anything to make a connection. Now when the grandkids think of how he connected, they remember the life and impact their grandad had on each of their lives. Whether they lived in the same city or were spread out a thousand miles away, Dave connected with his grandkids and left a big legacy of influence and hope.

YOUR ROLE

You have a choice. Your role, should you decide to accept it, is to offer help and hope to your grandkids at a time when they need you the most. Some grandparents choose not to. There are folks who visit every year and bring a few presents but are never known for anything much. When they're gone, they'll be described as *good people*, and that's about it. Their impact is negligible; their legacy is nonexistent. Most importantly, their grandkids miss out on something they can receive nowhere else.

You have a place in their life, even if you are as old as dirt. My encouragement is not to save the best for last. Start spending yourself now. If you don't feel like you connect with your grandkids, then love yourself into their lives by the way you listen, respond, and understand.

God has you in their lives for a reason. Find out what that is and make it happen.

Your Presence

No matter how much distance there is between you and your grandchildren, you can still leave a legacy of presence in their lives. Technology makes it easy to stay in touch. Get your grandkids to set up FaceTime or Skype on your computer, tablet, or smartphone. Don't be afraid to call, learn to text, or video call your grandkids anytime. When you know they're coming to see you, create an environment where rest and refreshment reign. Continue to love them when they're at their lowest. Invite them to be part of your life and let them know you are interested in theirs.

Even if you are having health issues, you can still share a very important part of life with them. Your gray hair means something to them, so take advantage of it. There are very few people involved in the lives of your grandchildren that can offer them the wisdom and insight you can. That will only happen through your presence in their lives.

Your Words

The words you speak are an expression of who you are. Truly, out of the abundance of the heart, the mouth speaks. What's in your heart for your grandkids? I hope it's love and acceptance, not criticism and judgment. Now, you don't have to like their attitudes or actions sometimes. But try not to let on. They get enough of that from others. Your words have the power to destroy, ridicule, demean, and crush. Or your words can encourage, support, uplift, and affirm. Be careful with your words, for they can be like a rudder that determines the direction and the ultimate destination of a great ship. Misspent words can always be forgiven but are rarely forgotten.

Make your grandchildren proud to be yours. Lift the spirits of your grandchildren when life is weighing them down. You can speak wisdom into the life of your grandchildren or allow them to fend for themselves in a world of information that will never really give them what they desperately desire.

Your Actions
What you do to engage with a grandchild will confirm or nullify the words you speak to them. Actions do speak louder than words, and the challenge for every grandparent is to make sure the words from your mouth match the actions others see in your life.

You can draw grandchildren to you by showing a spirit of gratefulness for your life and their place in it. You can push them away by complaining about where God has placed you. Know you are always being watched by eyes and heard by ears that will one day emulate what they see and put into practice what they hear.

Your Legacy
A great legacy is the result of a life well lived. The legacy you leave for your grandchildren has got to be intentional. You can be the greatest person ever to all your friends and acquaintances, but that doesn't matter if you fail your own family, especially your grandchildren. Take advantage of this unique relationship and be an irreplaceable lifeline to your grandkids. You can change the destiny of your family.

Another dear friend, James MacDonald, made a comment to me in passing (not the death kind of passing) that I immediately asked him to repeat. He was describing what their church, Harvest Bible Church, desired to be known for. His statement is a good one for every grandparent.

"To love without condition, welcome without judgment, and forgive without limits," James stated.

What will your grandkids remember you for? Your chocolate cake? Your criticism of the culture? How clean and uncomfortable your house was? Your negativity and ability to argue? Your love of scripture but hate for mankind?

Or will they remember how warm and welcoming you were? The way you handed them the control of every conversation because you wanted to hear their hearts? Those special experiences where you laughed out loud and had fun together? The times that you just happened to show up when they needed you the most?

How will they remember you? Will they remember what you left in their bank accounts or what you deposited in their lives? There's a big difference between what is written on your tombstone and the legacy you write on the souls of your grandkids.

My prayer for you is that when you close this book, you'll have some new ways to make memories and great reminders of how you should engage with your grandkids. As you put these tools to work in your family, your grandchildren will remember the preciousness of the time you spent with them. They'll recall the special relationship they've had with you, and how you gave them a taste of the character of God and the grace and hope He offers all His children (and grandchildren).

Your presence, your words, and your actions all work together to fulfill your role in creating a legacy of influence that will forever impact future generations of your family. That legacy will determine how you will be remembered by those who love you dearly.

May you walk with humility, demonstrate kindness by your actions, and love when you want to walk away. I guarantee if you do, you will make an impact on your grandkids and give them a lasting legacy of influence and hope.

Chapter 24

A LEGACY OF
RELATIONSHIPS

Therefore I intend always to remind you of these qualities, though

you know them and are established in the truth that you have.

2 PETER 1:12 (ESV)

I can promise you these three things: You're going to die sometime after you read this book. It's going to happen sooner than you think. It's not going to happen the way you want it to happen.

There's something about embracing the inevitability of life ending one day that has a way of focusing you on what is most important today. It helps you live smarter and look at each day as a blessing. Yesterday I went to a restaurant and the waitress asked me, "Are you celebrating anything today?"

"Yes, I am," I said. "I woke up this morning, and that's worth celebrating."

CELEBRATING WHO YOU ARE
AND WHAT IT'S ALL MEANT

If you're feeling that brisk fall wind of change ushering in a transition of the seasons in your life, then no doubt you are also wondering a bit about what your life has been about. You start to focus on what will be remembered about you once you are gone. Some folks don't care, and when they are gone, they will quickly be forgotten except for an occasional search on Ancestry.com or when some relative is flipping through old family photos.

Then there are those of us who want to pass something on. We want to know our lives meant something more than mere existence. We want to see how we made an impact on someone else. We want to make lives better and our time on earth significant. We want to know we made a difference.

I'm not sure I thought about this when my own kids were born. Jan and I were so ecstatic about having kids that we only thought about how we were going to survive. We were both twenty-one years old, managing apartments, going to school full-time, and working two jobs while leading a Young Life club for kids. When Melissa and Adam were born, we saw a miracle happen before our eyes. We never regretted having kids early, but we weren't focusing on our legacy back then.

When our grandkids were born, we encountered new feelings of getting older, wanting to make an impact, and thinking about life from a different perspective. Our kids changed the way we lived; our grandkids changed our hearts and our focus.

There was something so different about having grandkids that my whole perspective on life changed. It was no longer about making money, doing a great job, building a career, and involving myself in everything good I could find. It was more about impact, knowing these little kids I was holding, who would eventually call me Poppa, are the ones who would carry on any family legacy if there was going to be one. They were the hope for future generations of our family. It was then that I asked myself, *What do you want to be known for?*

Short of making the history books, setting records, or committing some heinous crime, most of us will be forgotten when our grandkids are gone. Our work may be remembered, something we wrote or videotaped may be read or viewed, but our legacy will only extend as far as our relationships with our grandkids.

Your legacy will be written in two places.

One is on your tombstone. Now, I don't know about you, but I don't know many people who run around cemeteries with the intent of gathering wisdom from the one-liners on tombstones. This headstone monument thing seems a bit overrated to me. People always ask me what I want written as my epitaph, like there are going to be thousands of people visiting my buried carcass to see what my life was about.

I wonder what will be on mine.

"Here's lies a guy who had a mustache."

"Mark was fun."

"Here lies a guy who sent us pecan pies at Christmas."

Can you tell I really don't care what's on my marker? I'm sure it will say when I was born and when I died, like all the neighbors planted in my new neighborhood.

My legacy will not be determined by my headstone.

Okay, I'm digressing a bit here, but after a funeral, when do you ever see a person's headstone again? When you're laying another family member to rest, but that's really not the best time to be searching for some tombstone wisdom. So I don't think too much about what will be chiseled about me after I'm gone.

The second place your legacy will be written is in the hearts of those who know you. In particular, those you have known.

THIS THING CALLED LEGACY

A legacy is not about depositing a few gold nuggets of wisdom that will be remembered by all. You're not a box of fortune cookies—clever but not very deep. A legacy is not just doing a whole lot of good for others. A real legacy is some meaningful characteristic or quality passed on from generation to the next along this bridge called relationship. A legacy is found within the hope and wisdom you passed down to your children and grandchildren, the truths they can pass down to the next generation. Grandparents who leave a legacy are not only remembered for what they contributed, but also for the life-giving qualities they provided to those around them. A legacy is not what you have left in their bank account, but what you have deposited in their hearts. And it all happens because of the relationship you have with the next generation as they see the importance of your life and those qualities that have now been passed on to them.

My main concern is not everyone out there. My main concern is the health and welfare of my own family. That's where I want to make the most difference, in the lives of my wife, my kids (including my son- and daughter-in-law, even though I can't tell the difference because I consider them all the same), and my grandkids.

I've been to many funerals, and it's interesting to see who attends. When my mom died, the people who attended were a few of her friends, a couple from her Sunday School, a couple of neighbors, and a few folks from some of the organizations where she volunteered. The remaining people there were all family. Our whole family was there. The attendance at funerals speaks loudly to the legacy that deceased person left for their family.

All the wisdom shared through your legacy, should it go any further than your life, will go as far as your grandkids or great-grandkids. That's good enough for me.

I'll leave it to the next generation to take care of their grandkids; I'm just trying to keep up with the four I have.

My point in all this is to ask you, "What do you want to be known for?" My real hope is you'll ask that question for yourself. Then answer it and live the answer.

WHAT DO YOU REALLY WANT TO BE KNOWN FOR?

I think about that when I'm introduced to people, run into acquaintances, and when someone introduces me to an audience before I speak. I've been described to crowds and individuals in so many ways that many times I chuckle and think, "Is this really how they see me?" At least a few times I've cocked my head and asked, "Is this really what I want to be known for?"

I was recently at a Texas Rangers baseball game and ran into a fellow named Aaron Watson. He's a country music artist and a great fellow. He introduced me to his wife as, "Honey, this is the guy who sends us that pecan pie for Christmas every year."

Many people just know me as "Jan's husband." Others introduce me as, "This is Mark, and he's the guy who lives with all those kids in East Texas." Some remember me as, "That guy with the mustache." Many of our Heartlight parents introduce me to their friends as, "He's the one I was telling you about who cooks those great steaks." When speaking at seminars or conferences, I'm known as, "That guy on the radio."

A few weeks ago, Amy Grant introduced me to her husband, Vince Gill. I was excited to finally meet him. Amy and Vince are warm, genuinely kind people. No joke—her introduction was, "Vince, this is the guy who lives with those struggling teens and has all those cabins that are joined by walkways." I'm not kidding.

I can see it on my tombstone now: "Here lies Mark, the pie guy on the radio who has a mustache and lives with all those kids, who is married to Jan and cooks a great steak and has cabins all joined by walkways."

Not exactly what I was going for in my legacy. Not quite what I want to be known for.

I know this: Legacy is all about relationships. Not just my relationship with my grandkids, but my grandkids' relationships with me. I want to know them, and I want to be known by them.

But having an impact on someone doesn't just happen because we know them, or when we do something that can benefit their life. It's all about relationship, about getting to know them and know them well. It's communicating life across a bridge of relationship that doesn't stop if they don't respond. It's offering your life to them regardless of what comes back to you.

THE TRICKIEST RELATIONSHIP

Family relationships are tricky. I've heard many families tell me they can all get along if they don't talk about religion or politics. Others tell me that, as long as they don't bring up other certain topics, then the holidays will go well. I've always thought relationships have to be more than that. Relationships, true relationships, don't need to be bound by restrictions but rather be freed up to flourish.

If you're going to have freedom within your relationships, then you might have to accept the fact that it's okay to disagree. At times you may be polar opposites, but your relationship can still thrive.

Your relationship with your grandkids can be the most important relationship they have during their teen years. Don't mess it up by requiring your grandkids to believe, act, and present themselves the way you do. The relationship is always the most important thing, because if you don't have a relationship, then you will never be able to have those much-needed discussions that might bring about a different way of thinking. You'll never have talks to disperse the wisdom you have accumulated. You'll eliminate the chance to have influence and opportunity to shape their thinking and mold their values.

Grandparents, even if you don't accept the lifestyle and choices your grandchildren make, don't *throw the baby out with the bathwater.* If you do, you won't have a chance to touch the hearts of those who long for your presence in their lives.

I can reject them and their lifestyles and never have an influence, or I can love them right where they are and hope to steer them in another direction. Again, accepting them does not mean that I accept their choices, lifestyle, behaviors, or actions. I'm not condoning when I don't correct. I can love them in spite of their behaviors. I know actions are an expression of their hearts, and that's what I want to influence.

Relationship matters.

Regardless of the differences of opinions or the inconsistencies in your beliefs, the relationships with your grandchildren matter. You can have an amazing impact on the lives of your grandkids even when your beliefs are miles apart because you are the one who can offer the hope and help they are desperately looking for. You have the ability to leave a legacy no one else can. Over that bridge of relationship can travel those qualities and memories that will build your legacy in your grandkids' minds. And in your children's lives.

Leave a good one, a legacy filled with family members who remember in detail the positive impact your life had on them. It's a pay-it-forward kind of thing. Just as others had an impact on you and changed your life, I'm sure you have a desire to have an impact on others.

Legacies don't just happen. They're made. Keep making yours today. If you haven't started yet, there's no time to waste.

ACKNOWLEDGMENTS

A special thank you to the following folks who have influenced the writing of this book.

To David Muth, Dave Tillack, and Smith Brookhart for providing so many lessons that I learned from you and for showing me how to do this *legacy thing* right. Rest in peace, my dear friends.

To Heartlight Ministries and all the staff who provide the perfect laboratory for me to learn about grandparents, parents, and teens. A special thanks to the Heartlight board of directors, Mike and Carol Barry, Andy and Lisa Deer, Jonathan and Meagan Pyle, Brad and Meghan Respess, and Brian and Dawn Tanner, for your friendship and help with making Heartlight a wonderful place for families and teens.

To the Heartlight Ministries Foundation for fulfilling the mission to offer help and hope to a broken world. A special thanks to the board of directors, Bill and Susanne Walsh, Roger and Lori Kemp, Jerry and Leanne Heuer, George and Livia Dunklin, and Alan and Belinda Carter, for your continued and much appreciated support.

To Bill and Gloria Gaither. This was your idea and how thankful I am for your suggestion to reach out to grandparents everywhere.

To Roger Kemp and Company, Wayne Shepherd, Joe Carlson, and K.T. Losie, for making our *mass communicatin'* a haven of hope and a place of blessing for so many parents.

To our kids, Blake and Melissa Nelson and Adam and Nicole Gregston, who allow us to be involved in the lives of our grandchildren.

And, of course, my wife, Jan, with whom I get to figure this parenting and grandparenting out. I wish I had had a grandmother like you.

ENDNOTES

1 Irene M. Endicott, *Grandparenting Redefined: Guidance for Today's Changing Family* (Aglow Publications, 1992).

2 Swindoll, Charles R. "Having Fun." *Today's Insight with Chuck Swindoll.* Christianity. com. 10 Feb, 2015.

3 "Nag." *en.OxfordDictionaries.com.* Oxford Dictionaries, 2017. Web 8 July, 2017.

4 "nagging." *Merriam-Webster.com.* Merriam-Webster, 2017. Web. 8 July, 2017.

5 "Rick Warren > Quotes > Quotable Quote." *Goodreads.* https://www.goodreads.com/quotes/601712-our-culture-has-accepted-two-huge-lies-the-first-is.

6 Swindoll, Charles R. "Having Fun." *Today's Insight with Chuck Swindoll.* Christianity. com. 10 Feb, 2015.

7 Swindoll, Charles R. *The Finishing Touch / Becoming God's Masterpiece.* Dallas, TX: World Pub., 1994. Print.

8 Kataria, Madan, (Kataria,1955). "I have not seen anyone dying of Laughter, but I know millions who are dying because they are not Laughing." 5 Jun, 2010. Tweet.

9 Sax, Leonard. *The collapse of parenting: how we hurt our kids when we treat them like grown-ups.* New York: Basic Books, 2017, p. 198.

10 Peter the Hermit quotes. Quoteland. http://www.quoteland.com/author/Peter-the-Hermit-Quotes/1599/.

11 Lewis, C. S. *The Four Loves* 1960 ed. New York: HarperOne, an imprint of Harper Collins Publishers, 2017. Print.